Looking Back to Tomorrow

RUTH PATTERSON

Looking Back to Tomorrow

A SPIRITUALITY FOR BETWEEN THE TIMES

VERITAS

First published 2009 by
Veritas Publications
7/8 Lower Abbey Street, Dublin 1, Ireland
Email publications@veritas.ie
Website www.veritas.ie

ISBN 978 1 84730 198 7

Scripture quotations are taken from the *Holy Bible*, New Lining Translation, copyright
©1996. Used by permission of Tyndale House Publishing, Inc., Wheaton, Illinois
60189. All rights reserved. Scripture quotation on p. 125 taken from *The Message*,
copyright © 1993, 1994, 1995, 1996, 2000, 2001, 2002. Used by permission of
NavPress Publishing Group.

Lines from 'For a New Beginning' and 'For Love in a Time of Conflict' by John
O'Donohue taken from *Benedictus*, courtesy of the Estate of John O'Donohue and
Transworld Publishers, 2007. Lines from 'Abraham' by Jessica Powers taken from
Twentieth-Century Apostles by Phyllis Zagano, courtesy of Liturgical Press, 1999. Lines
from 'The Rose' by Amanda McBroom, courtesy of Warner/Chappell Music Inc.,
USA. Lines from 'Little Gidding' by T.S. Eliot, taken from *Four Quartets*; lines from
'The Hollow Men' taken from *Poems 1909–1925*: courtesy of Faber and Faber Ltd.,
London, 1959; 1932.

Cover designed by Niamh McGarry
Cover image © www.imagefile.ie
Printed in the Republic of Ireland
by ColourBooks Ltd, Dublin

Veritas books are printed on paper made from the wood
pulp of managed forests. For every tree felled, at least one
tree is planted, thereby renewing natural resources.

For my niece, Mary, who is truly a bridge.

Contents

Introduction

A few years ago, I was asked to write a book on a spirituality for between the times. Too much was happening. There didn't seem to be the space or the time to embark on such a project. This year, Restoration Ministries, the organisation with which I work, has been taking a Sabbath year in order to reflect on our journey so far and where we feel God is leading us. As part of that year I was given a couple of months' sabbatical, an entirely new experience for me! And I felt the time was right to give it a go. I found myself very aware of the sense of bewilderment, confusion and hopelessness that so many people are feeling in this present time when confronted by personal grief, suffering and trauma, by community dysfunction, by the all-pervading economic crisis, by anger at political representatives who have betrayed the trust placed in them, by disillusionment with the Church, by the global fear of terrorism and by uncertainty about the future of planet earth. Apprehension, loneliness, pointlessness, depression, weariness and so much else tend to make people close in on themselves, build walls for self-protection or live in a shadowy world of unreality, rather than face a pain that might overwhelm them. The cry from at least some has been, 'In all of this – where is God?' Where is God when I am exhausted, rushing around caring for everyone else's needs, with no time to look to myself and no one to care for mine? Where is God when I am disappointed, let down, betrayed by someone I trusted and loved?

Where is God when someone close to me is suffering deeply and I am powerless to fix it? Where is God when I have lost someone or something very dear, maybe through the death of a loved one, the loss of a job, or the loss of reputation when I have been falsely accused, rejected and condemned? Where is God when I feel my body becoming frail, not doing the things I want it to do, and when I can't remember things that happened only yesterday, when the fear of dying, maybe dying alone, sweeps over me like a tidal wave? Where is God when I find myself in the place of temptation and discover that I'm on what seems like sinking sand, rather than the solid rock I was sure was there? Where is God in a Church where once there were so many certainties; we were told what to believe and accepted what came from those in authority over us, but now it seems to have lost its way? In this present age when that authority is questioned, because of the fallible nature of those in leadership and the sometimes seeming irrelevance of its witness, we don't know where to turn to find an authentic moral stand, a courageous prophetic voice or a vision bearer. Where is God when whole nations put themselves in the place that belongs to him alone and seek to exercise total power and control over the destinies of others? Where is God when that lust for power leads to the torture and death of countless millions of innocent human beings and the litany of atrocities and disasters from around the world grows longer by the day until we seek simply to block so much pain out of our minds, batten down the hatches and look out for number one?

I could go on listing so many dilemmas and questions with no answers that would satisfy the silent screaming inside us. How do we live in times such as these where we seem without solutions? Maybe it's not so much answers we're looking for as a sense of presence. In order to become aware of that Presence, it is necessary to pause a little, to take time, even for a few minutes each day, simply to be. As we practise doing that, we will gradually become aware that we are not on our own, that, in a way that is hard to define, we are being held, accompanied, comforted, called, challenged and above all loved. Hope is reborn, trust is strengthened and we are opened up to the wonder of the 'eternal now' as we walk along the road between the times. What this book will attempt to do is to point to some of the timeless truths from the storylines of yesterday that can nurture our spirituality in this present in-between time and link us to the tomorrow of that new creation, for which everything is groaning as in the pains of childbirth. Perhaps it will help us to be a bridge!

CHAPTER ONE

Between the Beginning and the End

We live between the times, but then that has been the lot of every man, of every woman since time began. The one thing that humankind can be totally assured of is that things and people, places and situations change. Perhaps what makes this era different, what heightens our uncertainty and can make us feel a bit disoriented is the vastly increased speed of change in so many areas of our living. Before we have time to become used to one area of change, another one creeps up on us unawares. We are taken by surprise and are unsure about which one to tackle first. What these changes might mean for our personal lives, our citizenship of our particular country, the future of the planet and of the human race itself is anybody's guess. As the people of God, our telling of the story, our living it out in this particular in-between time has not infused people with hope nor encouraged them to embrace this stage as a crucial and grace-filled moment. How can it if we don't know it for ourselves? How do we become catalysts to enable people to walk together again with God, walk together with themselves, with their fellow human beings in all their diversity and with creation itself? Where do we start in a world that so often seems hell-bent on self-destruction, where the rich get richer and the poor get poorer, where the Church increasingly appears irrelevant, where faith in Jesus Christ crucified and risen flags up a remnant rather than being that which addresses the hunger in so many hearts for meaning and fills the

God-shaped hole at the centre of their beings and at the centre of the earth itself? It is a huge challenge to accept the fact that the old forms of religious life and the practice of the faith as we have known it are declining. It is an even bigger challenge to let go, to embrace that decline in the conviction that the Holy Spirit is moving us towards something new which we cannot yet name. That's a hard place to be. Yet this is the reality of now. It is the lot of every religious order, certainly in the West, as it is also the lot of all those of every persuasion who profess to be followers of the Way. It is hard to welcome a dying process before you know what resurrection will be like. It is frightening and painful to let go when you cannot see something up ahead to grasp.

Some time ago I had a letter from a dear friend in Holland. He belongs to a religious order that is experiencing a similar decline. He is now in his eighties, having lived his vocation in many remarkable ways in different parts of the world. Recently my friend and his brother priests were all on retreat at their mother house. I quote: 'It was the last retreat we were able to have in the trusted environment we had known for so many years of high drama and ideals. Five months from now we are going to leave it since we can no longer live in it in the way we had been used to. We are going to move to a home for aged priests that will be more adjusted to our needs of the moment. An important period of our history will come to an end. It will bring pain to many of us. The house has been sold. The new owner will have it pulled down in order to put up a new project. The spots where many of us have taken their first steps on the road to their vocation will not be found anymore. Only one place will still be ours: the cemetery deep in the silent wood where a number of empty spaces will be awaiting our own funerals.'

Many of us facing a similar letting go will identify with this particular story. What was striking for me was the theme of their retreat – 'Looking Back to Tomorrow'. To look back meant to keep the memory alive of the road they had followed at God's behest. Looking back to tomorrow is another way of saying 'rediscovering our story'. And for the Christian pilgrim of whatever denomination, to rediscover our story means to rediscover Jesus Christ, crucified and risen. It means to walk together again with him and to realise that there is so much more yet to know of this Jesus who commands our loyalty, our obedience, our unconditional love. And the only way we are going to make a difference in our world, to offer a spirituality for between the times is, in a sense, to embrace the unknown in trust. It is to walk with Jesus, especially perhaps with the Jesus we don't yet know, befriending mystery, the mystery of Jesus and the mystery of ourselves at a much deeper level than we have risked heretofore.

For children, the words 'Once upon a time' are full of magic. They herald the start of a story that usually leads them into a land of wonder and excitement, a place where their imaginations are given full sway. The tales that are told may have a thousand different faces, but the underlying storyline is inevitably that of the triumph of good over evil, culminating for the protagonists in a state of 'happy ever aftering'. That's what children want to hear. It gives them a feeling of safety, a sense that this is how things should be. It creates boundaries in their minds about the rightness of certain behaviour, attitudes and reactions and the recognition that, if those lines are crossed, then chaos of some sort or other ensues. The unspoken assurance that all will be well allows their imaginations to take wing through myriad emotions, encompassing the scariest of events and the most unimaginable experiences to the final resolution that satisfies their sense of justice and fair play. They have a conviction that, no matter how things may seem, someone or something will rescue the one in distress or restore the one who has been cheated or elevate the underdog to a position of importance. No matter how many times the story is told, they live each moment of the drama as if it were being told for the first time. They know the ending, but they know also that each word is of crucial importance, put there for a purpose, part of the intricate weaving that will culminate in the final outcome, an outcome that will be good. They have an uncanny awareness of a phrase missed or a page skipped by an inattentive adult who has either lost the sense of wonder or is too weary to enter, yet again, into the drama. In all of this, the role of the narrator is crucial and awesome: to bear witness to the world the author has created and to lead the children through the experience from its beginning to its ending.

For people of faith, our 'Once upon a time' is 'In the beginning God'. Whatever interpretation we put on the first chapters of Genesis, whether we take them as a literal account of creation or the narrator's way of telling the story in order to reveal the essence, the nature and the activity of the Author, for us the veracity and the wonder of the words remain. They are built into our faith memory and herald the start of a story whose ultimate ending is not ours to determine, is not even known to the storyteller but only to the Author of it all. The scene is set before the start of what we call time, and these opening words never cease to thrill and excite us, 'In the beginning God created the heavens and the earth. The earth was empty, a formless mass cloaked in darkness. And the Spirit of God was hovering over its surface' (Gen 1:1). Act One of the great drama is about to unfold, the first spoken words being those of the Author himself. The hovering Spirit picks up the command, order emerges from chaos, light shines in darkness and progressive revelation begins. It seems as if the world of 'happy ever aftering' is here to stay. All is well. What has been created is declared to be good, culminating in the emergence of humankind, made in the image of the Author, male and female patterned after himself, and blessed above every other living thing. God looks at all he has created and sees that it is excellent in every way. In this Eden, this place of safety, there is harmony among all creation but it is upon man and woman that the stewardship of everything else is bestowed. To them also is given the most priceless of all gifts, that of communion, not only with one another but also with the Author himself. They are the beloved of his heart. He delights in relationship with them. The freedom of the garden and the gift of intimacy with the Creator are assured. For such a blessed order to continue, only one boundary is set in place, established out of a loving concern. The warning is given that if that particular line is crossed, then chaos of some sort or other will ensue.

The deed is done – inevitably, you may say. The line is crossed. The uninterrupted flow of intimacy is stemmed, childlike innocence is shattered, brokenness and vulnerability become the order of the day. The freedom and openness of loving communion are replaced by fear as Adam and Eve hide themselves. The question that has never needed to be heard in the garden before resounds throughout creation, 'Where are you?' The great alienation has begun as humankind, becoming aware of its 'nakedness' and in the resulting shame and fear, builds walls to defend and protect itself, a process that leads to exile from the garden and estrangement from the Beloved. In essence the storyline from that point onwards is a repetition of the question as God seeks again and again to restore the intimacy that was lost. With one or two notable exceptions the question is not answered because of the expertise in self-defence built up over aeons of time, as human beings acquire and perfect the learned behaviour of hiding their true selves.

We know the story so well for it is what has moulded us and shaped us – the story of the 'fall', of breakage, banishment, wanderings, second chances, homecomings, rebellion, exile and restoration until the time comes when God puts into action his master plan, the plan that had been in his heart and mind since before the creation of the world as the only way to walk together again with him in the intimacy that was there at the beginning of all things. When the time is 'right', God answers the question 'Where are you?' by coming himself. Once again the Spirit of God hovers, this time not over a formless mass cloaked in darkness but over a young girl called Mary. God speaks, the Word becomes flesh and light shines again in darkness as God makes our homelessness his home. The 'I love you' of God, embodied in the person of Jesus, is neither accepted nor understood by the majority of those still hiding themselves behind power and control, manipulation and greed. They plot his death, believing themselves to be in command, not recognising that every element is of crucial importance, put there for a purpose, part of the intricate weaving that will culminate in the final outcome, an outcome that will be good. The free and willing obedience of a God who becomes human, a God who refuses to hide, a God who is crucified in nakedness and vulnerability, a dying God who cries out to God from the cross, 'Where are you?' and receives no answer has turned the tables. He takes upon his sinless Self all that belongs to darkness so that we might once again find ourselves and be found in right relationship with God. And this is not only for ourselves alone but also that we might have the possibility of walking together again, in beloved community, with the whole created order. Death itself, as C.S. Lewis once famously put it, starts working backwards, and all things become possible. The end has become the beginning. In fact, what is the beginning? What is the end? Perhaps they are only our way of placing words in the storyline, a story that is still in the process of being told.

And we, as people of faith, as the Church, are the narrators with the crucial and awesome responsibility of bearing witness to the loving heart of the Author and leading others through to a recognition that they also are a vital part of this story. But it is not just 'others' who are crying out to be led through. We ourselves, who are supposed to have another dimension to our living, are also somewhat lost. We don't feel safe any more. We are afraid of intimacy. The old social and moral boundaries have disappeared. We are no longer sure of how things should be. We tend to equate the statement 'all will be well' with wishful thinking rather than with a vibrant affirmation of trust and hope. Someone may appear on the national or world scene who, for a time, rekindles our energy and expectancy, but this person cannot be the fairy godmother who magically transforms everything. The clock inexorably strikes twelve, they fall from the unfair pedestal upon which we have placed them and we return to the drudgery below stairs! There's no glass slipper waiting for the perfect fit, and happy ever after is the stuff of childish dreams. What's happened to the storyline? Have we lost the plot? How do we fulfil the calling of anointed narrators, we who are so often weary with life, we who by and large have lost our sense of wonder, who no longer stand on tiptoe in our spirits before mystery, who would long to skip a few 'pages' and concentrate on what we feel will simply get us by? And, just as importantly, where are those who will not let us do this, who care passionately enough to remind us that every moment can be an eternity moment for those who see, with the eyes of the heart, the unfolding love story of God?

My own spirituality has been nurtured greatly in the last few years by a statement made by Richard Rohr in his book, *Everything Belongs*. He says: 'We cannot attain the presence of God because we are already totally in the presence of God. What is absent is awareness. Little do we realise that God is maintaining us in existence with every breath we take. As we take another it means that God is choosing us now and now and now. We have nothing to attain or even learn. We do, however, need to unlearn some things.'[1] To rediscover our story perhaps means that there are many things we need to unlearn. Maybe part of what the last years have been about has been an unlearning of some things that we held very dear and believed were so right. Unlearning makes us feel uncertain and even vulnerable. It's a risky space to be in, a no-man's-land or limbo state, to admit that there is another way to live, another way of looking at things, a way forward other than the particular one we adhered to for so long.

It seems to me that there is no quick fix but rather that we have simply to remember redemptively the road we have followed already at God's behest, looking back in order that we may look forward to the unknown tomorrow, in order to allow ourselves to be seized again by that first love which captured our hearts, our souls, our lives. With that energy, we will be prepared to walk with and befriend the stranger, the Jesus we don't yet know, and allow him to befriend the stranger within us, the bits of us that we have not yet discovered or loved, the bits we have hidden because of any one of a hundred fears or doubts or inadequacies. In rediscovering Jesus we rediscover ourselves, our true selves; we rediscover our world in all its terrible and shining wonder, and we rediscover what has been there from the very beginning, though masked by greed and fear and lust (and perhaps most deeply by shame), namely a common humanity.

All we have is this moment, this now, but we so cloud and colour the present with our wounds and hurts of the past, and so mask the possibility of a bright tomorrow with our fears and anxieties for the future that often we miss the great importance of the present. This is our time and it is in this time that God calls us to be on tiptoe in preparation for what is yet to come. It doesn't matter if we cannot see or know what is up ahead. Today is preparation time for the future, for tomorrow, but this moment is also sacred. It is special and stands on its own. It is an essential part of the story. Without it, a vital 'phrase' is missing. How we bear witness to God-with-us and God-yet-to-come, how we live between the times is crucial. I believe that the only way to incarnate the story and so convey that sense of wonder is for us to take on board fully the fact that God is choosing us now and now and now. It is that awareness and that mystery that the anointed narrators live with and in – between the times. Long ago some of the very early followers of the Way were facing pressure and persecution. Times were extremely hard, leading some to question their faith and to be deeply worried about their future. The writer to the Hebrews encourages them by reminding them that Jesus is able to identify with all their pain and hardship. He urges them to follow the example of those people of faith who have gone before them and who kept on following in the midst of great trials. And then he gives them guidelines as to how to live in the present moment: to love each other with true Christian love, to show hospitality to the stranger, to remember those in prison, to share the sorrow of those being mistreated, to give honour in marriage and to remain faithful, to be satisfied with what they have, to remember the leaders who first taught them about God, to be willing always to find Jesus 'outside the camp', that is, beyond our own comfort zone, and to be people of hope. Through all of this, the phrase that shines out like a neon light is this: 'Jesus Christ is the same, yesterday, today and forever' (Heb 13:8). If we truly believe that, then it enables us to look back to our yesterday with courage, to live in the present moment with hope and to face the future with confidence.

Ray McKeever, whose song inspired the subtitle for this book, repeatedly asks the question, 'What shall we do between the times?'

We have acknowledged that between the times is a hard place to live out our vocation. In the song he looks back to a time when the river flowed full and clear, when there was a singer in each person and when there was a road that led to freedom. He contrasts that time with now where the river bed is dry and empty, where the sounds we make seem so uncertain and where people have no one to lead them. What do we do when the water's just a trickle, when the song is just a whisper, when freedom is imprisoned in our lives? He makes the affirmation of faith that those who trust the movement of the centuries can still see the river flow, can still hear a song to sing and can still walk along the road between the times.[2] Looking back to tomorrow? The truth behind these words is that there is nowhere that God is not. He is just as present in these seemingly chaotic times as he was when the world appeared to be more orderly, when people seemed to have more respect for themselves, for others and for the earth, when more people seemed to acknowledge his existence. We are always between the times until he comes again. Instead of viewing this current stage with apprehension, weariness or despair, perhaps we should turn our perceptions upside down and view it as a gift, as a graced time. It is John Bradshaw who says: 'We are not material beings on a spiritual journey; we are spiritual beings who need an earthly journey to become fully spiritual.'[3] What an unlearning is there! What an aid to seeing things differently (which is one definition of repentance!). If we are the ones called in this present moment to be carriers of the story, and if we ourselves are part of the story and part of the story is us, then the key to our spirituality lies in looking back to tomorrow. In essence we are a bridge between what has passed and what is yet to be. As we journey together my prayer would be for a deeper awakening to the truth that we are already totally in the presence of God and a heightened awareness of the fact that God is choosing us now and now and now.

Notes

1   Richard Rohr, *Everything Belongs* (New York: The Crossroad Publishing Company, 2003), p. 29.

2   'Between the Times', words and music by Ray McKeever, ©1990 Ray McKeever, 2415 East 22nd Street, Minneapolis, MN 55406.

3   John Bradshaw, *Healing the Shame that Binds You* (Deerfield Beach, FL 33442: Health Communications, Inc., 1988), p. 22.

CHAPTER TWO

Leave Your Own Country

After those clear, cloudless days that we are sometimes blessed with on the north-west coast of Donegal, I have stood gazing up at the night sky with its myriad pinpricks of light. There is a sense of awe and wonder in this threshold place where the veil that hides the other world that is all about us seems very thin, almost as if a corner has been lifted and, for an instant, in the eternal now, mystery that is more tangible than the earthly reality all around, is revealed. A barely perceptible breeze, like the sound of the gentle whisper Elijah heard at the entrance to his hiding place, or like the breath of the Spirit touches the skin, and God is very near. The human spirit is on tiptoe, on the verge of a great awakening. In this eternity moment awareness is given and, if received, life can never be the same.

Just so must Abraham have felt thousands of years ago as he stood under the night sky of Haran and looked up at stars too numerous to count. His father Terah, who lived to a great age, had had the notion of leaving his birthplace, Ur of the Chaldeans, to go and settle in the land of Canaan, but, instead, when he and his family reached the village of Haran, he decided to stop, to go no farther. There he intended to put down roots and there, so everyone thought, they would remain. Although they had not been blessed with children, Abraham and his wife, Sarah, had a comfortable life in this place that Terah had chosen for them as home. At this stage Abraham wasn't a young man. Perhaps he felt that most of his living had been done, that the dreams and adventures of youth, the hard work and consolidating of wealth and security that came with middle age were behind him. Nothing left now but to live out his old age in peace, surrounded by the respect, friendship and deference his life and position had won for him. And yet, 'Once upon a time, under a night sky in Haran, God spoke' and life for Abraham could never be the same, nor could it be for the entire human race ever since.

'Leave your own country, your kindred and your father's house and come to a land I will show you!'[1] Was it only a figment of his imagination or did he really hear a voice speak? Abraham waited, on tiptoe in his spirit, for somehow he knew there was more to come. 'I will cause you to become the father of a great nation. I will bless you and make you famous and you will be a blessing to others. All the families of the earth will be blessed through you' (Gen 12:2,3b). Surely this was wishful thinking, the stuff that dreams were made of! He was seventy-five years old. His wife was barren. How could this be? (A question reiterated centuries later, first of all by an elderly priest, Zechariah, and then by a young girl in Nazareth.) Abraham's spirit was on the verge of a great awakening. In that timeless now, awareness was given and Abraham obeyed. All the record tells us is simply, 'So Abram departed as the Lord had instructed him' (Gen 12:4). It doesn't tell us of the disbelief in his home community, or the ridicule from his friends, or the loss of respect of fellow elders or the grief of his father. It doesn't recount the emptiness of leaving the familiar behind nor the loneliness of being misunderstood. Abraham didn't know when he set out that the best was yet to be. Perhaps all he knew in those early years of pilgrimage was that his homesickness for a city designed and built by God was greater than the homesickness he felt for the village encampment of Haran, however dear its associations.

In his last book, entitled *Benedictus*, John O'Donohue, poet, pilgrim and prophet, has a poem for those who are embarking on something new. This 'beginning' assumes a persona of its own, quietly forming itself in the out-of-the-way places of our hearts, beyond our usual thought processes. It watches our desire for something more, feels the emptiness inside us grow and the struggle to try to let go of the old. It observes us playing with the seduction of safety and its accompanying lack of exhilarating purpose.

> Then the delight, when your courage kindled,
> And out you stepped onto new ground,
> Your eyes young again with energy and dream,
> A path of plenitude opening before you.
>
> Though your destination is not clear
> You can trust the promise of this opening;
> Unfurl yourself into the grace of beginning
> That is at one with your life's desire.[2]

It could have been written for Abraham. Whether he recognised it or not, somewhere in the quiet recesses of his being something must have been stirring, so that whenever he heard the call to pull up the tent pegs and come to an unknown destination, he was ready to hear and to respond. At age seventy-five, this was his moment of destiny! Having myself long since passed the sixty mark, that fact alone gives me great encouragement. Down through the ages, youth has always been regarded as a time of confidence, a time of trust, a time for adventure and courage, a time for exploring and building relationships, a time for crossing borders, trying new things, a time of enthusiasm, even of wonder. And that is true. But look at Moses who began his best work when he was eighty, at Zechariah and Elizabeth, at Simeon and Anna who all lived between the times, who nurtured their spirituality into old age and were ready when that awareness moment struck. They unfurled themselves into the grace of beginning and age didn't matter. What mattered was that this was their moment of destiny, that they were awake and didn't miss it. It is the moment, the awareness and the response that is important. If it comes at age twenty-five, so be it. If it comes at age seventy-five, so be it. If, within the gift of God, there is more than one awakening, so be it. It is said of Martin Luther King Jr. that if he had not had his defining moment, he could not have led the movement for civil rights in the United States. At his funeral, Benjamin E. Mays, President Emeritus of Morehouse College where King had been a student, declared, 'No man is ahead of his time. Every man is within his star, each in his time. Each man must respond to the call of God in his lifetime and not in somebody else's time – Abraham leaving his country in obedience to God's call; Moses leading a rebellious people to the Promised Land; Jesus dying on a cross; Galileo on his knees recanting; Lincoln dying of an assassin's bullet; Woodrow Wilson crusading for a League of Nations; Martin Luther King Jr. dying fighting for justice for garbage collectors – none of these men were ahead of their time. With them the time was always ripe to do what was right and that which needs to be done.'[3]

Abraham was within his star. The time was ripe – and right. No matter that he had been given an incredible promise, no matter that he set out not knowing where he was going, God knew what needed to be done, and for Abraham, that was enough. Abraham was faithful to the journey, so he received further revelation. The heart of God rejoiced in this man, in his obedience, his humility, his trust. Because of this faith relationship, Abraham could barter with God for the fate of a city and could surrender richer lands to his nephew, Lot. When the time came, he was even willing to lay down before God the life of his beloved son. It is through this steady, earthy record of trust that Abraham becomes known as our father in the faith. He encourages us to hear a different voice than the clamour all around us, to trust that a moment of awakening may come to us in as simple yet mysterious a way as a night sky or a gentle breeze. He proves to us that an individual who becomes aware of their moment of destiny and seizes it can make a difference 'between the times', can change the course of history. He shows us that trust and faith are possible even, or maybe especially, when it means leaving behind what has been familiar and dear, that which has to a large extent given us identity; and when what is asked of us seems too much to bear, he challenges us to an obedience nurtured out of a loving relationship. Above all, he calls us to pay attention to our pilgrim heart.

Throughout the ages the people of God have always been depicted as a travelling people, sojourners, those who did not have a permanent dwelling place here on earth because they were looking forward continually to their heavenly country. So they travelled lightly. Isaac and Jacob, heirs with Abraham to the same promise, were also tent dwellers. When Moses led the people out of slavery in Egypt they were pilgrims for forty years before they entered the land of promise. Jesus said of himself: 'Foxes have dens to live in, and birds have nests, but I, the Son of Man, have no home of my own, not even a place to lay my head' (Lk 9:58). He described himself as the Way. The early Christians were known as people of the Way, those who were pressing forward in faith and trust, those who were in the process of becoming what God had intended from the very beginning. Down through the centuries we have become more cautious. By and large, we are a settled people. We have our beautiful buildings, our structures and our carefully regulated ways of doing things. The Church has become a vast institution; in the West it is largely a vast, elderly institution that, with only some exceptions, stands in dire need of a great awakening. Institutions are very necessary. The danger comes when the institution becomes more important than its founder and the vision of the pilgrim church no longer excites our spirits or calls us to new ways of expressing the faith that is in us. It seems as if we not only have pitched camp at Haran, but have replaced pilgrimage with consolidation set in centuries of concrete! We are not happy to move unless we know exactly where we are going, have the resources to back us up and are sent on our way with the approval and admiration of our fellows. With declining interest in 'Church' as we have known it, the promise of a 'great nation' seems like wishful thinking. People may no longer be attracted to church, but they are still interested in God. They have, acknowledged or not, a spiritual hunger. They desperately need a spirituality that will empower them to really live in this now, which is all they have been given. For the soul of the Church to stand on tiptoe in the midst of mystery about to be revealed, to gaze at a night sky, to sense the gentle breath of the Spirit, to be willing to lay down what we have held most dear and to set out again, not knowing where we're going but trusting only that our pilgrim God is with us at this moment, seems to be the stuff of which dreams are made. And yet – and yet – could we, as the Church, but shrug off the baggage of 'old age' and pull up the tent pegs, what blessing would flow! Perhaps the crucial question is, 'Is our homesickness for a city designed and built by God greater than our homesickness for our particular religious comfort zone, however dear its associations?'

I dare not ask that question of others or of the Church, the beloved and, at times, wayward Bride of Christ unless I am prepared first and foremost to ask it of myself. Retrospective guidance is a wonderful thing! I can look back and see a number of defining moments when, almost in spite of myself, I did respond in the affirmative, albeit somewhat tentatively, fearfully and reluctantly. There are two, to date, that stand out more clearly than others. One was the call to ordination as a woman, at a time in Ireland when such a species was unknown! I was already trained and equipped to do other work that I enjoyed, and did not particularly want to hear a challenge that would take me on a lonely journey, far from familiar territory, to an unknown land. At the edges of medieval maps there used to be inscribed the words, 'Here be dragons'. Dragons there were aplenty on this pilgrimage, but the destination was reached, or so I thought! In reality, it was Haran! There I settled. The encampment became dear and familiar. Here, in this dispensation, so I thought, I would live out the rest of my days. It was a tough and enriching assignment, but as the years went by, unrecognised by myself, I too was 'playing with the seduction of safety and the grey promises that sameness whispered'. Once again, under some night sky the voice spoke again, 'Leave what has become your own country, leave what is, in essence, your father's house and come to a land I will show you'. The 'land' was Restoration Ministries, a non-denominational organisation for healing and reconciliation, birthed in the local church where I was minister but now grown too large to nurture along with a lively and needy congregation. I did not want to hear the voice. It had cost me so much to get in to the system. If people had not understood nor accepted the concept of ordained women, how in heaven's name were they going to understand or accept this? I pushed it away. I bargained with God. 'When you clear the debt on our church building, when you give us a base from which to operate and something for me to live on, I'll take these three things as a sign that I should go!' Then I sat back inside myself and said, 'Work that one out, if you can!' Still the voice persisted,

'Leave – and come'. Bargaining was recognised and confessed. At some point courage kindled. I left. Perhaps my Isaac in those days was recognised ministry within my own denomination. That, too, had to be laid down, before God, in his mercy, restored it. Words from Jessica Powers' poem on Abraham resonated with me very strongly, and still do:

> I think, alas, how I manipulate
> dates and decisions, pull apart the dark,
> dally with doubts here and with counsel there,
> take out old maps and stare.
> Was there a call at all, my fears remark.
> I cry out: Abraham, you old nomad you,
> are you my father? Come to me in pity,
> mine is a far and lonely journey too.[4]

And still do! What if there is another night sky with myriad stars, a gentle breeze touching the skin, another awakening, a moment of awareness that God is choosing me now and now and now? Would the question twenty years further down the line still evoke the same reactions and the same reluctant response? How do the scales of settler versus pilgrim weigh my homesickness levels?

There are many love songs in the Bible. One of the most beautiful is Psalm 45. It is addressed to the King, but half-way through the King himself speaks to his bride:

> Listen to me, O royal daughter; take to heart what I say.
> Forget your people and your homeland far away.
> For your royal husband delights in your beauty;
> honour him, for he is your lord. (Ps 45:10-11)

There follow the promises of blessings that will ensue. So it seems as if one of the chief tenets for a spirituality for between the times is to nurture our pilgrim heart, to be continually willing to let go, to leave and to come. I have yet to discover a better definition of pilgrim than that given by Phil Cousineau in his book, *The Art of Pilgrimage*. He suggests that one derivation of the word has its roots in the Latin 'per agrum' – through the field. 'This ancient image suggests a curious soul who walks beyond known boundaries, crosses fields, touching the earth with a destination in mind and a purpose in heart.'[5] There are plenty of biblical and more recent historical examples to back up that view. The way of the pilgrim is both an inner and outer journey, a journey of both the spirit and the body, perhaps the more crucial of the two being the inner. We have many unknown boundaries within ourselves, many areas of giftedness to be discovered and released, as well as hidden areas of shadow that need to be acknowledged and brought out into the light so that they might be redeemed, brought back into their proper place. Perhaps as we pay attention to our pilgrim hearts, a new and sanctified curiosity will seize us, as it seized Abraham, a holy urge to walk beyond previously clearly demarcated boundaries and cross fields, because we have a destination in mind and a purpose in heart. So often as followers of the Way, we have been afraid; our fear has immobilised us and we find all sorts of reasons, or excuses, for not going on pilgrimage, either inner or outer. But maybe we can only do that with confidence if we know, really know, that God delights in us, in our beauty, in what he has created. Out of that comes the courage to listen for the signs of the world that awaits us. At a retreat during Holy Week, 2009, Jean Vanier, now eighty years old, said this: 'To discover "I am because I am loved" is the most intimate identity. I am because I am loved by Jesus, by God, therefore I am not afraid anymore because I trust in this intimate relationship with Jesus. I don't know where that will take me, but somehow it will bring me back to this Jesus who offers me something radically new.' And as we step out in obedience, that obedience honours our Lord.

What will make our eyes, the eyes of the Church young again with energy and dream? When did we, as the Church, last stand in wonder under the mystery of a night sky dotted with myriad promise-holding stars, or feel the gentle breeze of the Spirit upon our skin, and know, in a place beyond normal knowing, that this was our defining moment? It is. It is this now that we have been given. Can we trust the promise of this opening, even though the destination is not clear? A new beginning is always grace, is always a gift. It is we who make it so complicated, when the reality is that all we need to do is unfurl ourselves into it and let the wind of the Spirit fill the sails of our pilgrim hearts. It is then that we know that this laying down, this leaving, and this coming to a land God will show us is at one with our heart's desire.

Notes

1   All scripture quotations taken directly from the Bible are followed by the relevant chapter and verse notations. All other biblical quotations, such as in this case, are subject to the author's phrasing.

2   John O'Donohue, 'For a New Beginning' from *Benedictus* (London: Bantam Press, 2007), p. 32.

3   Coretta Scott King, *My Life With Martin Luther King Jr.* (London: Hodder and Stoughton, 1970), pp. 369–70.

4   Jessica Powers, 'Abraham' from Phyllis Zagano, *Twentieth-Century Apostles* (Collegeville, MN: Liturgical Press, 1999), p. 67.

5   Phil Cousineau, *The Art of Pilgrimage* (Berkeley, CA: Conari Press, 1998), pp. 13–14.

CHAPTER THREE

The Wilderness

The wilderness is not an easy place. We can all talk about wilderness experiences, especially after we have come through them, but when we're in the middle of them, that is quite a different matter. The wilderness tends to be the term we use when we are searching for some way to describe those harrowing, inexplicable, honing times in our lives when we'd rather be anywhere else than where we find ourselves. These are times when there don't seem to be any answers for the questions raised, chief among them being, 'Where is God?' The wilderness can be the place of temptation, of desperate struggle, where light and darkness clash within us, where we can be seduced into thinking we have no choice and the way our natural desire wants to take us can look so plausible, so inviting and so reasonable. It can be the place of madness where we don't know what life is about anymore, where we're beset by so many fears, anxieties, unanswerable questions and nightmare scenarios through which somehow we've got to keep going and yet don't know how that will be possible. Sometimes it can be the place where we are hungry, so hungry for meaning, for someone to make sense of what is happening either within us or around us, hungry for justice, for right relationships, hungry for intimacy, for someone simply to let us know that we matter, that we are loved just as we are. It can be the frightening place where we have lost our way and don't know which path to follow, where every journey we make appears to lead us in a circle back to the same place of entrapment and there don't seem to be any signposts anymore. Certainly there are none marked 'Home'. There is no guiding star and hope is at a low ebb, if it is there at all.

The dictionary definition of wilderness is a desert, an uncultivated and uninhabited region. That immediately conjures up a sense of bleakness, of isolated exposure, of acute loneliness. Perhaps loneliness is one of the chief characteristics of the wilderness. To be alone and to be lonely are two different things. Sometimes we crave to be alone and that state can be a positive and enriching one. To be lonely is rarely positive. It can go as deep as the dereliction Jesus experienced on the cross. It can be a feeling of searing, aching loss or abandonment. I believe that Jesus deeply felt both those things – aloneness and loneliness. Often he felt the need to get away from the crowds and even from his close followers and friends to be alone – with God. These were the times when his 'batteries were recharged', when he communed deeply with his Father. They were also preparation times for what was up ahead. Those periods of aloneness were very important and necessary. But he also experienced loneliness, mainly at the times when people, especially his friends, failed to understand the journey he had to make. On one particularly poignant occasion many of his followers turned away and deserted him. What he had been saying was too much for them, too hard. He then turned to his twelve disciples and asked, 'What about you? Are you going to leave me too?'

Aloneness, without anyone or anything else, and the periodic need for it in what are, for many, very busy lives, we can understand. There is a sense in which we have a choice about it and sometimes actively seek it in order to regain our peace, to assess a situation, to reflect or to pray. Out of that being alone there may come a little more wisdom, a little more insight, discernment and peace. The experience can be positive and enriching. Loneliness is a very different matter. None of us are strangers to such a state. My mother is, at the time of writing, in a nursing home. Each day whenever my sister or I visit we are greeted with the words, 'Oh, I'm so glad to see you. I'm so lonely'. And there is absolutely nothing we can do to remove that feeling. While not literally without companions – there are other residents but their nearness doesn't deal with the difficulty – somehow part of the loneliness, part of her wilderness is that nearly all her contemporaries are dead; her memory is failing and she doesn't remember the visits she does have. While this can be also deeply distressing for us, we cannot walk this lonesome valley for her. I have another friend who at the moment is losing her memory. From being a bright and very competent person, she has moved into a world of fear and extreme loneliness, and nobody else can walk this path for her. Both my mother and my friend are in a very specific and fragile in-between time. All that those of us who love them can do is to seek to be present with them and to pray for Presence for them. Sometimes we can be at our most lonely when we are surrounded by people because what we are living at that particular time, we cannot share. We may wrongly assume that they have got their lives together and we are out on a limb where no one would understand. One of the loneliest places to be is in a married relationship that has broken down or is teetering on the brink of severance. But there is also the loneliness of the single person who longs for the intimacy of close companionship and family of their own. There is the loneliness of new immigrants, far from home and all that is familiar and dear, and that of all strangers in our midst. Or there can be the loneliness of being misunderstood, or falsely accused and deserted by those we trusted, with the accompanying feelings of low self-worth, rejection, abandonment, even betrayal. Whatever the cause, most of us at some point in our lives will have been in such a wilderness. We will have experienced dark places with no light shining and in those times we can't even conceive that a day will dawn when things will be any different. We are without hope and maybe even feel without God. I say 'feel'. Thank God that faith does not depend upon feelings that can, at times, be so fickle. For me, on a journey that often seems to be more in the wilderness than out of it, the real meaning of faithfulness is not so much that I cling on to God but that God clings on to me!

I defy anyone to read – in the right spirit – what are called the final discourses of Jesus, as they are recorded in St John's gospel, and not be deeply moved. Taken seriously, they are transforming words. Jesus had so much to say to his disciples before he left them. He knew that they wouldn't be able to take it all on board. In fact he actually says to them, 'Oh, there is so much more I want to tell you but you can't bear it now' (Jn 16:12). If that was so, then we have to believe that for that time, those last few hours, these words were the most important things he had to say. They were what would hold them in the in-between time of wilderness that was up ahead. Not a word was wasted. If they were instructions, challenges, warnings, affirmation and, above all, a declaration of undying love for his friends, then they are the same for us. In one of these eternity moments, Jesus is telling them about his pilgrimage, where he has come from and where he is going, and they respond with the words, 'Now we understand and believe that you came from God' (Jn 16:30). Jesus' response hovers in the air between them: 'Do you finally believe? But the time is coming – in fact it is already here – when you will be scattered, each one going his own way, leaving me alone. Yet I am not alone because the Father is with me' (Jn 16:31).

When I reflect on some of the very toughest times in my life, times of aloneness and of loneliness, when I did not sense any presence at all, there was always somewhere a faint, almost inaudible whisper within my being, 'I am not alone because the Father is with me'. That did not make the situation any easier to bear at the time, although there was the rather stark and solitary comfort of affirming it against all evidence to the contrary. But afterwards I could look back and know that it was true. Thomas Merton, modern-day mystic, heard these words and wrote them down, 'I shall lead you through the loneliness, the solitude you will not understand; but it is My shortcut to your soul'.[1] While we would not wish these times on ourselves or anyone else, it is true that when we emerge we can find that we have been given the treasures of darkness, riches that we could not have acquired in any other way. We have entered a greater awareness, a deeper relationship with God and we know that there is no turning back. But these are journeys that no one else can make for us. They are trials we must face ourselves, and no one else can take our place. And that's hard, very hard. Those who love us have often to stand back and watch helplessly.

When everything seems bleak, when fear twists in our gut like a knife, when it doesn't feel as if there will ever be any good solution to our particular nightmare, it would be easy to over-spiritualise the experience and, in so doing, partially deny the reality of what is happening to us. Having said that, if we can reach the point of recognising that this is where we're at, of naming our condition, our perception may change. We may discover that it's not so much answers that we're looking for as a sense of presence in this wilderness that has either invaded our beings or is surrounding us like a wasteland. We know that there is no easy way out, but even the faintest whisper that we have not been totally abandoned, that we are not fully alone is enough to enable us to see things differently, albeit, at first, barely perceptibly. The scene around us changes, ever so slightly, and there is a dawning awareness that the wilderness itself has something to offer us, that it is not all negative. When Jesus spoke those words from John 16 to his friends, he added, 'I have told you all this so that you may have peace in me. Here on earth you will have many trials and sorrows. But take heart because I have overcome the world' (Jn 16:33). He doesn't say, 'If you believe in me everything is going to be great, no problems, no difficulties, no tragedies, no wilderness experiences'. Rather he says, 'It's going to be tough, really tough, but lift up your hearts, take courage, be assured – I have already (not at some point in the future – but already) overcome the world'.

So it appears the wilderness is not the totally uninhabited and uncultivated place it first seemed, that there are things hidden, waiting to be revealed, things that will nurture our spiritual beings as we walk along the road between the times. For example, it can be the place where God gets our full attention. After living the pampered and advantaged life of a prince in Egypt, Moses, his cover blown, spends forty years in Midian as a hired shepherd. One day, seemingly just like any other day, he leads his father-in-law's flock deep into the wilderness near Sinai. This is his defining moment. This is what all the previous years have been about, both his life lived in the public gaze where he was made aware of the responsibilities of power and leadership, and his hidden wilderness time tending unruly flocks. God gets his attention through a bush engulfed in flames, yet not burning. He steps aside to see. God speaks and after initial protests and extreme reluctance, the resulting holy ground of calling, commissioning and envisioning becomes Moses' consuming passion for the rest of his life. Throughout all the ensuing odyssey, the confrontations with Pharoah, the flight from Egypt, the crossing of the Red Sea, the forty years of wilderness wanderings, seeking to mould an often rebellious flock into a holy people and lead them into an awareness that they had been chosen for a purpose, God is always choosing Moses in the now. And God, the I Am, the One Who Always Is seems to select the wilderness to accomplish some of his best work with the beloved of his heart!

It is in the wilderness also that God can satisfy our hunger. He gives us food for the journey – enough to keep us going. For the Israelites who complained to Moses that they were going to die of hunger in the desert and that it would have been better had they remained as slaves in Egypt, he provided manna to sustain them during forty years of wilderness wanderings. For Elijah, fleeing in terror from Ahab and Jezebel after his confrontation with the prophets of Baal and praying that he might die because he'd had enough, a messenger from God provided him with bread and water to give sustenance and strength. Indeed the messenger returned a second time, saying, 'Get up and eat some more for there is a long journey ahead of you'. Elijah travelled forty days and nights until he came to the cave at Mount Sinai. It's worth noting that in both instances the wilderness mentality had crept into their spirits, their complaints summed up in the question, 'Where is God? Why did he let this happen? It would be better to be dead than be in this state!' 'Forty' really signifies a long time. God is the God of the long haul and, often unacknowledged by us, his provision sustains us for the journey that would otherwise prove too much for us. Led by the Spirit, Jesus, at the start of his public ministry, went into the wilderness. He was there for 'forty' days, during which time he was relentlessly put to the test by the Devil. This particular wilderness, which stretched from the central plateau of Judea to the Dead Sea was known as Jeshimmon, meaning devastation, a place of almost unbearable heat, of jagged rocks and dust. During all this time Jesus ate nothing and was very hungry, desperately so for bread, but even more to hear God's heart for the way ahead. This was not the only time of temptation for Jesus, but right at the beginning of his ministry it was a bit like a rite of initiation, a time of hard testing, as he wrestled with the method he would use to proclaim the good news. It was in the wilderness that Jesus' mission statement was forged. It was out of the wilderness that he emerged in the power of the Spirit in order to become for us the Bread of Life. It is the awareness of that reality that can sustain us in our particular Jeshimmon, for we may still have a long way to go.

Having said that, it is important that we do not stay in the wilderness longer than is necessary. For a time, perhaps a long time, we may have no choice. It has not been of our making, or we may have been driven there and it has become our hiding place, eventually turning into a rather uncomfortable 'comfort zone' – like Elijah's cave. In the aftermath of cataclysmic events, fleeing in terror from those who had sworn to kill him, this cave is like the security of the womb for him. He's a physical, emotional and spiritual wreck. He curls up in a ball of exhausted self-pity, but he can't escape from God. 'What are you doing here, Elijah?' What a crazy question – or is it ? Elijah has to come out of the cave, voice what he is feeling and then wait for the answer, an answer that doesn't come in the way he expects it to, not in earthquake, wind or fire, but in the sound of a gentle whisper. It's not an answer either that he wants to hear. He's told to go back the way he came, into the centre from which he fled. But as he emerges, he will find there a different reality than the one he had built up in his mind; he will find that he's not the only one left, that there are many of the faithful who will stand with him and are awaiting his return. It's a new day for Elijah and his fellow Israelites.

It's a new day for us in Northern Ireland. We have had nearly forty years of wilderness. Amidst all the chaos God has been very present, has got our attention more than once, has given us food for the journey and now we are on the edge of the fulfilment of many promises. It's a crucial time. There are many who have got used to 'desert life', even to the negative identity it has given them. The uncomfortable comfort zone is better than taking risks which might mean forfeiting things that either they still carry from enslavements to old attitudes or the influence, kudos or recognition that they may have carved out for themselves during the desert time. There are those, like the Israelites, who would choose a leader and go back to the old ways. There are others who simply want to hide from the challenges, like Elijah, largely through a sense of weariness or impotence. But thank God for those who have been faithful to the wilderness journey, and who know that they are called to look back to tomorrow, to be, in themselves, a bridge between the times.

The wilderness times in our own lives are more than enough for us to deal with. We move to another level when we consider the Body of Christ. What has happened to us, we who call ourselves the Church? For a long time throughout history churches were full. But today, certainly in the West, as we look around at declining numbers and lack of interest and energy, we might need to be asking the question, 'Who or what were we following?' Were we simply following the tradition into which we were born, the one that nurtured us in the faith (and it has to be said that many did an excellent job with the highest of motives and great integrity) or, while valuing and respecting our tradition, were we really following Jesus, growing in relationship with him, so that he became the most important person in our lives? Were we believing in him and believing him to such an extent that we were prepared to follow him into strange territory, to take our stand, even at the expense of popularity and reputation for the sake of the gospel values of mercy, justice, truth and peace? Did our traditions teach us that the most important commandment was to love, to love God with all that is in us and our neighbours as ourselves? Or did they firstly look to building walls of protection so that doctrine and dogma were safeguarded? I am not knocking doctrine or dogma. They are very important and keep us from straying into erroneous or way-out beliefs that can over-emphasise one aspect of the Christian faith at the expense of so much else and so produce a deep-rooted sectarianism or isolationism that bears little of the hallmarks of Christian community.

Maybe it is 'way-out' to say that the heart of the gospel is love. If it is, then I want to be way-out. Jesus said, 'If you want to be with me, to come with me, then you must love me more'. More than what? Is one of the reasons that the Church seems to be in the wilderness just now because we have loved other things, even very holy things, more than him? And what would it mean for us collectively and individually to love him more? Paradoxically, it might push us out into a different wilderness, but perhaps in that place we would find ourselves again. Jesus said, 'You cannot be my disciple if you do not carry your own cross and follow me' (Lk 14:27). Is one of the reasons that the Church is in the wilderness just now because we have not understood the cross and what it means to carry it? We have taken lesser things and called them, almost blasphemously, our cross and have spent so much time and energy carrying them, things that he never meant or asked us to carry, that we have no faith or strength left to carry the true cross that he asks us to bear for a broken community and a weary, wounded world. Is one of the reasons the Church seems to be in the wilderness just now because we have sought to be and to do by our own strength rather than by his, because we have felt the need to present an image of success, of being in control, of power and we are now on the defensive because, in so many places, that long-preserved image has come crashing down and the accusations of betrayal of trust, of lack of authenticity, of hypocrisy and irrelevance follow thick and fast? Maybe we need this wilderness to discover again that we are not called to success but simply to be image-bearers of Jesus. Perhaps it will be in the wilderness of this present age that God will woo us back to himself, so that we will become aware of how much we are loved and how we are called to let other people become aware of this also. It could be that the wilderness is a gift to us where we realise that all along we were being called to a place of belonging in order to help other human beings discover the source of their being. That source is no other than Jesus himself. But we cannot help others do this unless we rediscover him for ourselves. Maybe in this wilderness there will be a new meeting, a new encounter that will not vanish into the sand, but will grow and blossom and flourish, bringing hope and courage because we are no longer afraid of letting our vulnerabilities, our littleness, our weaknesses be seen, for we have entered into covenant relationship with Jesus and so our very brokenness, our common humanity can become the place of communion – new Church!

Salt is good for seasoning. When did we last have flavour? When were we, as the body of Christ, an absolute necessity of life for people? At what point did we slip over the boundary into the weariness, the boredom, the human expertise of keeping the machine going rather than being something that gives zest, taste, challenge, wonder, energy and enthusiasm for the upside-down Kingdom of God, whose values we proclaim but whose life so often declares the opposite? Where is God? I make the affirmation of faith that he, too, is in this wilderness, searching for us, wanting, not our plans and projects, but our hearts. He's in love with us, so much in love that he gave everything for us. He's not going to abandon us here, but maybe he's allowing us to be here for a while until we rediscover just how much he loves us and just how much we love him. When that begins to happen, then we can begin to leave our wilderness place with joy. When we realise how much we are loved there will be a transformation in us. Love always transforms. In the Song of Songs the question is asked, 'Who is this coming up from the desert, leaning on her lover?' (Song 8:5). A transformed Church will be recognisable by the fact that she is leaning on her Lover, a Lover who is none other than Jesus himself. Then people will take notice. Those who have been disappointed by Church, by 'believers', will be wooed back, not to an institution, not to a dogma, not to a doctrine but to Jesus the Beloved One. And who knows what will happen next?

Note

1   Thomas Merton http://www.wccm.org/images/PDF/VV6A4.pdf.
       p. 13.

CHAPTER FOUR

The Prophetic Voice

I am not a particular fan of reality television but it cannot be denied that it holds great attraction for millions of people. Programmes such as *The Apprentice*, or *Britain's Got Talent,* or *Big Brother* seem to capture the public's imagination. Perhaps part of the appeal is that those who audition for such shows and risk going public, with all the ensuing pressure, excitement and potential fame or shame, are by and large ordinary people like us. What has given them this extraordinary publicity and has aroused such interest is that, at a time in the history of the world when so much is uncertain, when people are losing their jobs and their homes due to the enormous economic downturn, when the dreams of so many have been shattered and the ordinary person doesn't seem to count or be noticed – here, from their ranks, have emerged people who have dared to dream. They have been willing to step out, to risk ridicule to make that dream a reality and, in so doing, they have been bearers of hope.

On 4 November 2008, on a very different stage than that of reality television, the first black American to become President-Elect of the United States of America delivered his victory speech. It was broadcast around the world. In what Barack Obama called a defining moment heralding change, he referred to the enduring power of American ideals, one of which was unyielding hope. 'While we breathe we hope, and where we are met with cynicism and doubt and those who tell us that we can't, we will respond with that timeless creed that sums up the spirit of a people: yes we can.'[1] In the subsequent 'honeymoon period' people from the far corners of the earth, as well as many of his own fellow citizens, have been looking to him, hanging on his every word. Why? Because he is in himself, by virtue of his parentage, a bridge; because he has given people a sense of dignity and worth that they have never known before; because he speaks the language of freedom, opportunity, unity and hope. He has given them the freedom to dare to dream again. The 'yes we can' philosophy has, temporarily at least, released something in people that can act as an antidote to the insidious and destructive poison of negativity and despair that characterises so much of the present era.

Throughout their history the people of the Old Testament fell into many dark holes, largely through their own rebellion. Their chief sin was probably either self-reliance or looking to other earthly rulers to protect them or save them from invading enemies. Once they did that, the door was open for many other things and desires to take the place of God in their lives. There was only one name for that – idolatry, which was anathema to the God who had chosen them and loved them and whose desire for them was that they should be the ones through whom his purpose for the whole earth would be fulfilled. But God never gave up on them, no matter how much they wounded his heart. Time and again he called unlikely people who walked closely with him to be a prophetic voice, to speak out, not of their own hopes, dreams and desires but those of God himself. He did this, trusting that one day the people would listen and really hear, would see things differently and turn back again to him. We know now that, despite a faithful remnant who kept on waiting and hoping for God to come and deliver them, those who were called the 'quiet in the land', drawn largely from the ordinary people rather than the ruling classes, it was those with influence, those with power who stoned the prophets and killed those God sent to them.

The people of the Old Testament longed for a prophetic voice, yet when the prophets didn't say what they wanted to hear, they stoned them. They longed for the Messiah to come and yet when he came, they killed him because he wasn't what they expected the Messiah to be. Today we long for someone who has that sort of prophetic voice which will give us hope, like those of long ago who heard God's voice and fearlessly proclaimed his message, even though they never lived to see its fulfilment. They had courage to speak out about what was going to happen hundreds of years down the line because they were prisoners of a hope that, somehow, they knew would not be disappointed. They dared to dream. Throughout the ages we have never been totally devoid of a prophetic voice. What characterises each one of them is this unyielding hope.

Such a one was Isaiah of Jerusalem, who lived just before the time the people of Judah were taken into exile. 'No matter how things seem at the moment,' he tells them, 'there's going to come a time when a great light will shine for those who are currently walking in darkness or living in the land of shadows. It will emanate from the most ridiculed and despised part of the country, from Galilee. The form that this light will take will be in the birth of a child, such a child that the world has never seen nor will ever see again. Ultimate power will rest with him, and the hallmarks of his unending reign will be justice, fairness and peace. No one name will be able to encapsulate all that he is, but some of his royal titles will be Wonderful Counsellor, Mighty God, Everlasting Father, Prince of Peace.'

Isaiah could only proclaim this because it had been given to him by God. He knew the passionate heart of his God, a heart that was breaking out of love for his people. He knew that, no matter what the people did, God's commitment to them would never fail, because his love was a covenant love and would not be broken from his side. But it must have been hard for Isaiah to speak out what was being revealed to him, when all around him was disaster and despair. These words were given not just for Isaiah and for his day but for all time, words of hope and encouragement, announcing something so fantastic and unbelievable that there were many who would simply have scoffed at them and disregarded them, rejecting the prophet along with his message.

The prophets of doom appear to have the loudest voices these days. All around us are people weighed down by burdens, trapped in prisons of their own or other people's makings. When we look farther afield and dare to begin to absorb some of the unspeakable things that are happening right now in this torn and broken world, we might be excused for questioning, 'Where's the glory? Where's the hope? When did we last see a light shining that had an inextinguishable aura about it? When did we last hear the fearless voice of a prophet, someone of unyielding hope who could inspire others, not with an easy optimism but with faith that the promises she or he proclaimed would be fulfilled, not because they said it, but because they had taken the time to listen to God and knew, in a place beyond normal knowing, that those promises would be fulfilled?' A collapsing world economy, serious climate change, futile and seemingly never-ending wars are having a spin-off effect on everybody on this planet. Through all of this there comes the call to trust God. In the words of Isaiah of old, 'Do not think like everyone else does. Do not be afraid that some plan conceived behind closed doors will be the end of you. Do not fear anything except the Lord Almighty. He alone is the Holy One. If you fear him, you need fear nothing else. He will keep you safe' (Isa 8:13-14a). I would dare to add, in all humility, a postscript: 'If we trust God for something, then we trust him for everything, or we trust him for nothing.' It's easy to say, but much harder to put into practice. Maybe we need to begin practising, not only for our own sakes but so that others whom we encounter every day, those who are walking in the darkness of some deep trouble, might catch a spark of hope and begin to believe that changes, growth, even miracles are possible. Can we dare to dream again?

Micah was someone who dared to dream. He lived hundreds of years before the birth of Jesus. He was an ordinary working man who lived in a small town. His home country of Judah was facing a crisis of life or death proportions, and was lacking the moral fibre to deal with it. He had been gifted with the power of discernment and, like all the other prophets throughout history, when he saw what was happening, he could not keep silent. No matter that in the eyes of the world he was a nobody. No matter that in the eyes of the powerful, the village of Bethlehem, of which he spoke, was of no account. What Micah 'saw and heard' he proclaimed. 'But you, O Bethlehem Ephratha, are only a small village in Judah. Yet a ruler of Israel will come from you, one whose origins are from the distant past' (Mic 5:2). With this amazing announcement there came also the promise of homecoming after exile, followed by a description of the chief characteristics of this promised leader. He would lead in the strength of the Lord, in the majesty of God. Around the world his name would be honoured and he would be the source of their (and our) peace. Needless to say Micah did not live to see the fulfilment of this prophecy, but he was a person too of unyielding hope and his words took root among the quiet faithful of the land.

God is so often the God of surprises! Time and again he chooses to act through the little and the seemingly powerless. Although they don't recognise it, the powerful of this world are as clay in God's hands. The mighty Caesar Augustus and King Herod the Great didn't know that they were as puppets in the plan of

Almighty God. They were not the principal players on the stage of the greatest drama ever to unfold on this earthly stage. Those who were vital to the fulfilment of the prophecy were a young peasant girl called Mary and a carpenter named Joseph. It was in them that God found the sterling material he needed for this moment of destiny for the world. Their simple faith, their humility, their loving obedience, their very hiddenness and even their vulnerability were the qualities he needed. To these two 'little' people he could entrust the beloved of his heart, his only Son. Who would expect the Saviour of the world to come in such a little way? Who would expect him to live such a 'little' life, largely confined to the tiny and despised province of Galilee? Who would expect him to die such an ignominious death, 'little' and alone? Who would expect him to overcome the final destroyer and to rise, triumphantly it is true, not to the blast of trumpets and the accolade of kings, but in a garden to a woman weeping and in a room above an inn where his followers were hiding, confused, terrified and ashamed, and on a shore to the Galilean fishermen who were to take his name, his message to the ends of the earth?

So often, in the face of the enormity of events, most of them seemingly catastrophic, that are happening in the world today, we could fall into the trap of thinking that there is nothing we can do to make a difference. Even in more local scenarios – in our communities, our churches, our families – we can be paralysed by the thought that we can't make it right. Who are we to think that we could be used as instruments for change, as signs of hope? Thoughts like these can very readily put us on the slippery slope of thinking that we are no use, that we aren't worth very much and that we've got no particular gifts or talents that could be of use to others, let alone to God. Bethlehem didn't set itself up to be a special place. It did receive some kudos from being the birthplace of King David, but that isn't what has kept its name alive throughout history. Micah was an ordinary, unknown man who had no pretensions to greatness but in the midst of national crisis and his ongoing daily labour he took time to listen to God. His relationship with God forged him into a person of unyielding hope who was able to proclaim the word of the Lord to an entire nation. Joseph was a small-town carpenter who found himself faced with a sharp, two-edged surprise. Because he was a man of deep faith, he chose the road less travelled. His choice and his obedience helped change the world for ever. Mary questioned her destiny, but she did not question God. Her response, 'I am the Lord's servant and I am willing to accept whatever he wants' (Lk 1:38), has become the model for all those who, in humble obedience and loving faith, choose to place their trust in God, no matter how things seem. 'He has taken princes from their thrones and exalted the lowly. He has satisfied the hungry with good things and sent the rich away with empty hands' (Lk 1:52-53).

So it seems that God rejoices in littleness! It seems he would rather work through those who are small and weak and vulnerable, who are willing to let God be God. It seems that the key to their being chosen by God lies not in their position, or their economic prosperity, or their academic prowess, or their race, or their gender or their religious affiliation but in their relationship with God. It lies in the fact that they have discovered the amazing truth that it's not so much what we do as who we are that is important. If we know that the biggest thing God wants us to discover in life is just how much he loves us, and if we begin to tap into that, then something is released in us that simply allows us to be available to the Beloved, to God – and we will want to respond because we love and we are loved. We will also discover, as someone has said, that 'God doesn't call the qualified; he qualifies the called!'

I suppose that the loudest cry wrenched from the heart of all the troubled places in the world, and there are so many, is for peace; peace that is more than an absence of conflict, but that embraces compassion and truth and right relationships and is even more than all of them put together; peace that is the shalom of God, total well-being for individuals, communities, nations, and indeed the whole created order. That may sound like pie in the sky – this beloved community for which we yearn, yet will never see this side of death. But if we have chosen to stand on the side of the prophets and with the anguished peoples of this earth then we must give ourselves to it, and we must dare to dream. Such dreams are not daydreams. They are given for a purpose. They are not given to the faint-hearted. The song, 'The Rose', gets to the core of it:

> It's the heart afraid of breaking that never learns to
> dance,
> It's the dream afraid of waking that never takes the
> chance,
> It's the one who won't be taken that cannot seem to
> give,
> And the soul afraid of dying that never learns to live.[2]

We can dream all we like and be passive, but if we are willing to take the chance, if we dare to waken up, if we give ourselves to the dream for peace in the sense in which I have described it, if we learn to live by being willing to die for some of the things we have held so dear, if we dream passionately, then it has to be said that dreaming is dangerous. It will lead us along a path often marked out by loneliness. Sometimes it will push us to the edges, the edges of society, of what is accepted, and even to the edges of our own reason. Have we a dream that we are so passionate about that we are willing for our hearts to be broken? That's what it's going to take, if it has not started already in us, for there to be a new Ireland

and a new world. There is an enormous cost, a price to be paid for daring to dream in such a way, to be prophets of hope and makers of peace and, in order to do so, we too need, as did all the prophets before us, an encounter with God.

What is the dream? Is there a dream at all? Do we have a longing or an aching deep within us for something to happen, and can we put an image to it? What does it look like? It may be very faint, hardly discernible, but it's there. Perhaps we would love it to be rich and vivid in colour and in imagery, one that would be so direct that there would be no ambivalence about it, no mistaking it. Very often that's not the case, and we have to live with our dream for a while until it becomes part of us or we become part of it. Unless it is beating in our hearts, kindling our spirits, urging us on to new ways of bringing into being what we passionately believe God intends, however impossible that intention may sometimes seem to us, then the dream can become a nightmare that enslaves us rather than a clarion call that liberates us. There is a world of difference between dreaming passively and daring to dream passionately. Imagination is a gift from God, and sometimes the way we dream is to imagine the world differently (and then afterwards seek to bring that into being by what we do). When we dare to be open enough and vulnerable enough to receive the vision that is being given, then we need to articulate it, to announce it, for it has the power to bring about transformation in attitudes, practices and structures. To truly dream has little to do with deciding, without any reflection, what our and everybody else's agenda should be and then seeking to impose it upon them. To dream is, rather, to somehow learn the art of abandonment out of which something new is then free to emerge. We dream in the darkness, and our most prophetic dreams are treasures mined from dark places. It is often out of times of deep pain or anguish or prolonged weariness that we can suddenly be startled or grasped by vision. I would say we're pretty ripe for it right now!

Someone speaking about Martin Luther King Jr. said that his dream was to create a beloved community, a community at peace with itself. If that is so, if that is the goal, then the means, the method, the way must be one of love. The deepest desire in the heart of God, God's dream, is that we might know ourselves to be his beloved, and that this country, these islands, this world might become, as he intended from the very beginning, the beloved community, a community at peace with itself. If that is his dream, is it ours, and bearing in mind that we are not called, as someone has put it, 'to care for old ashes, but to kindle a new fire', what language would we put to it? How would we articulate it?

Dreams like these are never half measure, or mean, or miserly, or poverty stricken. They are rich and full of vibrancy and colour. Have the dreams we dare to dream in this in-between time something to do with seeing beyond today's pain, arguments, difficulties, tragedies, agonies and injustices to a time when we all understand one another better, when we agree to share at least a common humanity, when we're able to listen to one another and understand one another better, where we've learned to love ourselves a little so that we may love our neighbours much? If these are the riches, the sweet-smelling fragrance of the dream that we passionately 'march' for, then are we prepared for the cost? Many throughout history who dreamed of such riches ended with an assassin's bullet: people like Abraham Lincoln, Mahatma Gandhi, Martin Luther King Jr., Oscar Romero, or more recently, Brother Roger of Taizé, stabbed to death as he was about to lead an ecumenical prayer service. But the assassins did not kill the dream. The bullets didn't quench the fragrance or annihilate the vision.

We know these things because of Jesus. He had a dream that drove him hard. It made him set his face like flint for Jerusalem, where the cost for him was to take upon himself all the sin, the suffering, the anguish, the evil of the world, to embrace the cross, for the sake of the dream's realisation – the triumph, the victory of love. St Paul could write later with total conviction, 'He is our peace who has broken down the middle wall of hostility between us'.

Jesus told a story once about the cost of the dream that God's Kingdom might become a reality here on earth. 'The Kingdom of Heaven is like a pearl merchant on the lookout for choice pearls. When he discovered a pearl of great value, he sold everything he owned and bought it' (Mt 13:45-46). What is our precious pearl? It seems to me that I need not one, but many defining encounters with the Creator and the Giver of the dream in order to travel along that road of abandonment of all else, so that I might passionately become a prophet of hope, join in the dance of reconciliation and live the dream for peace. Perhaps the only thing, in the midst of so many unexpected and expected costs, that can keep me going, is to come to at least some limited understanding that to Jesus I am a precious pearl, that he gave up everything in order to own me, that, in a sense that is way beyond my comprehension, I am, we are, his dream. We are embraced already between the times by mercy, by truth, by righteousness and by peace in the person of Jesus, and are therefore already empowered to be prophets of hope and to be part of the dream's fulfilment.

Notes

1   US President-Elect Barack Hussein Obama's victory speech at Chicago's Grant Park, http://www.mainstreamweekly.net/article1021.html

2   'The Rose', Amanda McBroom, Warner/Chappelle Music Inc., http://www.amcbroom.com/rose.html.

CHAPTER FIVE

Exile and Homecoming

I had just turned twenty-one when I left Ireland to study in Canada for two years. One of the conditions of the scholarship granted me was that I remain in this country of my choosing for the full duration without returning home between the times. The reasoning behind this rule was eminently sensible, right and proper, namely that participants would get to know something of the country to which they had gone – its people, its culture, its geography, its traditions, its politics. For the most part, with the enthusiasm of youth, I embraced this wholeheartedly and lived it to the full. But there were periods when I experienced acute homesickness, when I felt myself to be in exile. At those times there would be within me a yearning and an aching for old, dear, familiar things, or for cherished relationships. Such moments could catch me unawares, sparked perhaps by an Irish accent or a piece of music, or a particular time of year, like Christmas or family birthdays. And I would long for the sound of a beloved voice, or the smell of the turf smoke in Donegal, or a taste of my mother's wheaten bread! It was then I would question why I had inflicted such banishment upon myself and the thought of homecoming would become very precious. I would conjure up what it would be like – the whole immediate family there at the airport to meet me, the reunion, the celebration. Reality is often different from our imaginings! The trans-Atlantic flight was delayed, resulting in my missing the domestic connection. The family had been at the airport but, wrongly informed that there would be no more connecting flights that day, had returned home. Instead of a rapturous welcome at the airport, I was met off a bus in the centre of Belfast by a couple of family members. We were all weary and somewhat subdued; however, needless to say, the welcome back was total and unequivocal. Even today, four decades later, I look back to those two years as one of the most formative and enriching periods of my life. Exile it may have been, but it was an exile that prepared me in ways I could never have imagined for what lay so imminently ahead for us all in Northern Ireland. I came home to the heady days of civil rights, so soon to be followed by the violence and the resulting abnormal society that shaped all our lives for more than thirty years and, on a different level, continues to do so to this day.

Perhaps one of the best-known exilic periods recorded in history is that of the captivity of the Jewish people in Babylon in the sixth century BC. Around about 538 BC, some of the exiles, under the goodwill of the Persian emperor, Cyrus, had begun to return to Jerusalem. They had spent many years in exile. They returned to find a city in ruins, their beloved Temple destroyed, and those who had remained demoralised, apathetic and fearful. Exile had filled them with anguish, homesickness and desperate longing. The homecoming, so long anticipated, redoubled their pain and grief. Imagine, then, those with some initiative left calling a meeting, maybe among the ruins of a deserted building, to look back at what had happened, to take stock of where they were and to wonder what sort of future awaited them. Those who had been in exile would have had different memories from those who had been left to survive in the debris of their once splendid city. Their assessment of those whom they deemed 'Enemy Number One' would have caused some dissension, some blaming the Edomites who in 587 BC had rejoiced over the destruction of the Temple and the city. Others would have laid all blame on the Babylonians, who were the chief perpetrators, who had slain so many and carried all those with any influence off into exile. The psalm that sums up some of this enormous grief, hatred and desire for revenge is Psalm 137. It expresses their absolute allegiance to their Jewish faith and to the God of their fathers, and their undying love for their country, especially for Jerusalem and their cherished Temple which they believed was the dwelling place of God himself. All were victims; all were survivors. Each had a story. Those returned exiles, having gone through the trauma of capture, imprisonment and relocation, might have felt their experience worse than those who had not been taken. Those who remained would have exhibited their emaciated bodies, their extreme poverty and degradation as evidence that theirs had been the harder lot. In looking back at what had happened, they would all have recognised a basic truth, namely that the sacking of Jerusalem and their total defeat had been the worst event in their history. Their interpretations of the event might have differed, but they would have shared common underlying negative emotions. Imagine at this point, someone with still some leadership qualities, a returned exile, taking the floor. He would have started with a lament, where he would have reminded his hearers how, as exiles, they had sat down (the traditional posture for mourners) by the rivers of Babylon. All they could do there was to weep as they remembered how life had once been. In response to the taunts of their captors to sing some of the songs of Zion, their only reaction was, 'How can we sing the Lord's song in a strange land?' The lament soon would have turned into cursing; first, a curse on himself if he ever let his love for Jerusalem grow cold, or forgot what their enemies had done, and second, a curse on those enemies of the most graphic and horrendous nature. In human terms this reaction was normal, so traumatic had been their experience. But they lacked that quality of awareness. They had much unlearning to do but did not realise it. They had no recognition of a God who was everywhere, ready to respond to his people whenever they turned to him. Rather their image of God was that of a God who was territorial, confined to Zion. They couldn't therefore sing in exile, or if they did it would be in the form of a lament. They couldn't express gratitude in their songs, because those songs of praise were sung as they ascended the hill of the Lord to the Holy Place; and even for those left behind, the Holy Place had gone. Nor could they announce any message, other than that of vengeance, because they hadn't realised that whether they were exiles far away from their native country or beggars at home where before they had been 'princes', they still had a choice. They could still choose to fulfil their destiny as the people of God, which was to be a light to the nations. Ruined places, ruined lives were their lot and unless someone came along to help them restructure their imaginations or facilitate them in how to view what had happened in a different way, this was the way they would remain.

How did they live between the times of exile and homecoming, between arriving back to waste places and the restoration that was demanded if they were ever again to be a people with an identity? Despite having been told by God through the prophets to embrace their captivity, to build houses, plant crops, raise their families, in other words, to really live as opposed to merely existing in the land to which they had been banished, they largely spent their time looking back to a questionable golden age or forward to the day they would return to Jerusalem. Many of them missed the lessons exile could have taught them – perhaps chief among them being the importance of the present moment and that even in exile God was choosing them now. Upon returning, they entered a different type of captivity, that of demoralisation, weariness, depression, dissension and apathy. Into the midst of all of this, there appears a man called Nehemiah. His is a remarkable story of how one person's vision, integrity and total trust in God can inspire a whole community to restore waste places, to rebuild out of ruin and to rediscover their faith. Physical devastation, low morale among the people, and those seeking to exploit the situation for their own ends were some of the problems he faced. Because he was a prayerful, deeply sensitive person, he was able to discern the difficulties and what needed to be done. But he also knew that he had to be open and honest before God, confessing that the whole nation had sinned, including himself and his family. The outcome of all of this was a strategy to withstand opposition to their work and to get at least one stage of the task completed. The key lay in Nehemiah's spirituality, which had been forged both in years of exile and in the raw, difficult yet wonderful times of homecoming.

Being in exile can conjure up many different images for us: a long absence from our own 'place', unfamiliar territory, living in an alien culture, having no one who understands where we're coming from, being cut off from family and friends, no sense of feeling at home, having no sense of belonging or identity any more, being stripped of much that gave life meaning. Exile can be geographical. It can also be, for example, the loss of a job that had been central to your life for a long time. It could be a physical or a mental illness that has removed you from relationships and involvements that were so important to you. It can be the vulnerability of extreme old age, in a nursing home, knowing that the only homecoming ahead is death. In such states, and many others, it is easy to assume that a sentence has been imposed and that there is absolutely nothing that can be done to alter the situation. But actually, there is one freedom left and that is the freedom to choose how we react to the situation. Do we choose, in so far as we are able to exercise choice, to use this time for the well-being of those among whom we have been placed? Can we see it as a time to exercise a generosity of spirit, to build bridges, to act with integrity, to seek to understand the other, to turn the other cheek, to bless rather than curse, to be bearers of hope? It's easy to say and much harder to do, but Nehemiah discovered the secret. His reactions to captivity were such that he was noticed and soon was given a position of great trust; a fact that eventually led to his being able to return to Jerusalem. If we are searching for a spirituality that will empower us in these in-between times, then one of the main keys that will unlock the secret of how to journey lies in our reactions to the situations we find ourselves in or to the conditions that life dumps on us.

In Northern Ireland we have emerged from decades of violence. The exile that those years imposed on us is over, but the homecoming to a place where all are welcome is slow to materialise. Ruined places and ruined lives are still in evidence. The same is true for other places in the world that are just now stepping over the threshold from the exile of internecine strife to the homeland of peace. Those people of faith who have been gifted with being able to live lives of both action and reflection need to be asking the questions, 'How did we live the times of captivity? Did we miss the lessons exile could have taught us?' These are fragile times. So much is possible, but we are also vulnerable. People have been through a lot. They are tired and their worn-down state can easily lead to the abdication of responsibility for building peace, lack of interest in things that are life-giving, depression and sometimes suicide. There's a huge legacy left from the past that needs to be dealt with through listening and the exercise of hospitality, as well as through prayer. Nehemiah used the old foundations of the walls to rebuild the new. There is much in our past that is good, that we do not have to throw away but rather take and remould and recognise for the precious treasure that it is. There are other bits that are rubble that we don't ever want to come together again, things like sectarianism, suspicion, fear of difference, bitterness. Like Nehemiah, we need a strategy in order to cope and to withstand such opposition. Obviously, we need prayer warriors constantly on guard. Perhaps what we need above all else is a spirit of forgiveness, a keen awareness of our reactions to people and events, a generous heart and a sense of gratitude, first and foremost to the God who has brought us thus far and also to all those who, throughout the years of exile and in this precarious homecoming, have lived with vision and integrity and total trust in God.

In contrast, being 'at home' has a completely different set of images. In 1994, Marty Haugen wrote a song that could be the anthem of any house, or community, or church, or country, that is seeking to be a place of hospitality. It is called 'All are welcome in this place'.[1] This 'house', which is a place of safety for all, has as its hallmarks forgiveness, love, faith and grace. It embraces hopes and dreams and visions. It makes space for the prophetic voice, for word and action that have no credibility gap. It enables those who come to dare to risk because right at its centre is the symbol of the biggest risk ever undertaken in the history of humankind – the cross. It is a place of table fellowship, of peace with justice, where the eternity moments of the unconditional love of God are beamed into the now of our existence, so that they begin to veer more towards being the rule rather than the exception. Here are found those who reach out in healing, serving, teaching and incarnating the Word, and right alongside them are the image bearers of Jesus – the poor, the marginalised, the most vulnerable. There is no more fear or danger, for each one is called by name, has an identity, is no longer orphaned. The songs from their broken places are heard and treasured and recognised as part of the living fabric that has shaped them into who they are. Here there is freedom to weep and laugh, to pray and sing, and the common refrain flowing through everything is, 'All are welcome in this place'.

Again, the saying of the words and the actual living them out are two very different things. As people of faith we aspire to the vision expressed in the song – a vision that beckons, but we're not there yet, maybe not remotely there. Every so often however, we catch fleeting glimpses of what it could be like, that is, we catch glimpses of the Kingdom. Eternity breaks into time and somehow we know, in a place beyond formal knowing, that immeasurable welcome flowing from the generous heart of God, not just for us, not just for the exile, or the stranger or those who are different, but for the whole created order.

Although we have entered a new and challenging era in Northern Ireland, we still have what are incongruously called 'peace walls'. Their function is to keep one side separate from the other. The motivation is fear of attack and that fear is fuelled by ignorance. Had the two communities not been strangers but rather had built relationship, then the violence that has been the experience of both communities would not have reached the momentum that necessitated, so it was thought, the building of the walls. As in the outer world, so it is in the inner. Whatever name we put on the 'community' that dwells within us, there are some parts that we are relatively happy with and other parts that we either refuse to acknowledge or else banish from our consciousness. We, in effect, build a peace wall so that we do not need to meet or greet the enemy within. These exiled parts do not go away. In times of heightened tension or great stress they can come out into the open, clamouring to be heard, to be given a voice. These 'strangers' need not necessarily be the frightening or destructive forces that we imagine them to be. They may be any one of a hundred things, like loneliness, or feelings of inadequacy, or rejection, or a deep-seated anger, or fear of difference, or a desperate need to belong – to name but a few. We may have spent our whole lives to date avoiding any meeting with them and so never discover that they may hold for us hidden treasures. If from somewhere we find the courage to welcome the exile back, that can be the point where healing begins. As we trust enough to enter the darkness, the secret places of our being and bring them out into the light, we discover more about ourselves and, because we have not gone there alone, even though it may have seemed like it, we discover, too, more about God. It is as if we are welcomed into our true identity. If you like, we are called by name, maybe truly for the first time in our lives. Out of that comes a respect for ourselves and a compassionate understanding that allows us to extend further hospitality. So the journey 'home' to our true self continues. As we begin to recognise that there is within us a place of safety to which the exiled parts of us can return, as we begin to give serious attention to the separation within us, then, slowly, the peace wall comes down. We are given glimpses of a new community where all are welcomed, heard, taken seriously and, therefore, do not have to express themselves in ways that are self or other-destructive. We become people of hope. We are being transformed from peace lovers into peace makers. Some of the poor and broken parts within may never be mended but we learn to accept them and live with them in such a way that they, too, can be a message of hope and something to celebrate rather than hide. To live the reflective life in the midst of busyness, great uncertainty, and the ordinary and extraordinary events that constitute our daily living between the times, is the quality that will enhance our spirituality. Dialogue with God, dialogue with the diverse parts of my own inner being and dialogue with the 'other' encourages the peace walls to come down, bridges to be built and homecoming to be experienced. Where there is such freedom of movement, 'to-and-fro' relationships are built both in the inner and outer worlds that will hold when crisis or difficulty next strike; and strike they will, that being the nature of these in-between times in which we live. No matter what conflict situation we look at in the world, there always comes a time when people have to 'come home', to pick their way back over the devastation and the anguish of the years and say to one another, 'All are welcome in this place'.

In this life that we often refer to as a journey, there may be one or many lesser exiles and homecomings. Through exile, if we so choose, we may learn valuable lessons to equip us for another stage of the way. We can also discover that the homecomings for which we yearn are not always easy, for they carry with them new responsibilities and may also incur the jealousy of those who do not want to 'welcome us back'. At several points in scripture the people of God are referred to as exiles, their true homeland being heaven. Therefore, it would seem that the greatest exile, and paradoxically, the greatest gift to our spirituality, is our life on earth. Whatever the duration of our time spent here, we are called, not to hide ourselves away, but to embrace this life wholeheartedly, to experience something of this world in which we've been placed, its people, its geography, its culture, its traditions. But there are times when we can feel an acute homesickness, a yearning and an aching for something that we cannot put into words, except to sense that there is something more. Therefore, it would seem that the greatest homecoming is when we reach the end of this life on earth. We cannot be homesick for something we have never known. Deep in our spiritual psyche there are memories of home. Our earthly journey has all but obliterated them from our consciousness, but they are still there. When this particular homecoming takes place, there will be no equivocation. It will be pure joy, unstinting celebration. We have come from God and we are going back to God. T.S. Eliot puts it this way:

> We shall not cease from exploration
> And the end of all our exploring
> Will be to arrive where we started
> And know the place for the first time
> Through the unknown, unremembered gate
> When the last of earth left to discover
> Is that which was the beginning.[2]

Notes

1   'All Are Welcome', text and music by Marty Haugen, © 1995 GIA Publications, Inc. 7404 S. Mason Ave., Chicago IL 60638.

2   T.S. Eliot, 'Little Gidding', *Four Quartets* (London: Faber and Faber Ltd., 1959) p. 48.

CHAPTER SIX

The Time Has Come

Whenever we think of Advent and Christmas, the image that most readily comes to mind is that of light shining in darkness. We have little problem with that. It is what happened. The narratives surrounding Jesus' birth are full of stars and angels and blazing lights in the night sky. The strange thing is that not many people seem to have noticed it – Mary and Joseph, a few shepherds and some travellers from the East who had been studying the stars. Hundreds of years before the prophet Isaiah had foretold that 'The people who walk in darkness will see a great light – a light that will shine on all who live in the land where death casts its shadow' (Isa 9:2). He prophesied that war would end and peace would reign. Isaiah looked into the mystery of the future and saw with the eyes of the Spirit that this light would come in the form of a child. That was part of his message. It is part, but only part, of the story of Advent and Christmas. We tend to take it and make it the whole. We focus on the baby, the little Lord Jesus asleep on the hay. We decorate every conceivable space with lights and gold stars, silver stars, and stars that are every colour of the rainbow. Our angels that appear on Christmas trees and lamp posts look more like Flower Fairies than the strong and mighty messengers of God coming to announce the greatest happening the world has ever seen or ever will experience. We become sentimental and do all we can to cosy up the story, to make it the ultimate comfort zone once a year. Bright lights surround a manger of sweet-smelling hay. Shining halos hover over the heads of the little family of three. And we're taken in, seduced, right up until midnight on Christmas Eve, or maybe until about ten o'clock on Christmas morning. Then, what we mistakenly call reality begins to seep into our spirits like a cold, damp, clinging fog that will not lift, even though we keep up appearances until the festive day is over. Don't get me wrong! I love Advent and Christmas, especially Advent, with all my heart. I delight in the Advent calendar and the poinsettias that have such a beautiful legend attached to them and point us to the wonder of the Holy Night. I love planning surprises for people. I relish the extra freedom people seem to have for a few precious weeks to be a little bit more open and demonstrably loving. I appreciate the cards that have been carefully chosen with a real Christmas message. I love the hospitality of meals shared and friendships cherished. I love giving and receiving little gifts. All of this is good, provided we remember why we are celebrating and the reason behind the preparation and the feast. I hate the pushing and the shoving, the grabbing and the getting, the over-satiation with food and gifts that leave people feeling exhausted, lonely and spiritually empty. The sense of being cheated manifests itself in the statement we hear so often, 'I hate Christmas!' It's as if there's a huge disappointment. Once again, deep within our beings, in a place known only to God and ourselves, we've missed out on something we really wanted. Our heavenly 'Santa Claus' didn't turn up with the one gift that would have made all the difference!

Perhaps we experience the let-down because we focus on only half of the promise we find in the prologue to St John's gospel. We have taken the first phrase and, metaphorically, put it in neon lights, have 'billboarded' it within our beings: 'The light shines through the darkness' (Jn 1:5a). Praise God that it does! But what happens when we can't see it? What happens when it doesn't appear, when the darkness gets deeper, when the night around us closes in? How do we keep journeying when there is no guiding star? What do we do when death casts its shadow within us or around us, or when evil seems to triumph over good? How do we deal with the death of a loved one, the agonising illness of someone dear to us, the severing of a relationship that we had believed was founded on a bedrock of unbreakable trust, the loss of a job with the accompanying crashing self-esteem and self-doubt? How can we get our heads around things like famine, drought, oppression, war, torture, pandemic disease, most of which could be halted if people opened their eyes and their hearts, if they became more generous and more vocal for justice? Was Isaiah merely a deluded fool? Was the content of his prophecy more about wishful thinking than being grasped by a vision, one that flagged up the true reality, the reality of the upside-down Kingdom that God gave birth to in Jesus? How could Isaiah say: 'His ever expanding peaceful government will never end. He will rule forever with fairness and justice from the throne of his ancestor David. The passionate commitment of the Lord Almighty will guarantee this' (Isa 9:7). How could John, centuries later, proclaim the same promise in different words: 'The light shines through the darkness and the darkness can never extinguish it' (Jn 1:5). The darkness can never extinguish it. The two phrases need to be held together always. There are many times when we cannot see any light shining, but that does not mean that it isn't there. That does not mean that God has turned off the switch. That does not mean that he is in the business of conserving divine energy! The power that God released through the Word he spoke in Jesus is something no other power, however strong, can overcome. The light that was turned on in Bethlehem can never be put out by any darkness, however all-embracing or deep. And this promise carries with it a guarantee. Isaiah names this guarantee as 'the passionate commitment of the Lord Almighty'. God's commitment to humankind was and is so huge that the only word that even approaches describing such a mystery is 'passionate'. That is not a head word. It's a heart word. It's a love-making word. It's a word that describes intense feeling. Put that word alongside commitment and, even then, we can only catch the merest glimpse of what God desires for us. It is so intense that he gave all of himself, everything, his dearest and best so that we might walk along the road between the times with confidence and trust, no matter what.

Advent is probably the one word above all others in the Christian faith which evokes the sense of an in-between time. It somehow holds past, present and future together. We know that at a specific point in history God has come to us, has visited us in Jesus. We affirm by faith that he is present with us in this moment. We believe the promise that he will come again, at a time God has appointed, to bring all things to their completion. So we live between the times of his coming and his coming again. The first Advent was the moment to which all of history had been looking forward. It is also the moment to which all those with the eyes of faith look back. It is the defining moment, one that is rooted in time and yet one that transcends time. From the point that God entered history in the birth of Jesus, his beloved only Son, nothing, absolutely nothing could ever be the same again.

You might be thinking, 'Well, what has changed? It seems as if we never learn the lessons of history and keep making the same mistakes over and over again. What was the purpose in Jesus coming if so many people still do not believe in him, if evil still seems to triumph over good and cynicism over expectant faith?' How many know what Advent means any more? How often have we been accused (and it's no longer a joke) of trying to push religion everywhere, even into Christmas!

When Jesus came, St John tells us that, 'In his own land and among his own people he was not accepted' (Jn 1:11). The world created by him, didn't recognise him. But that doesn't alter the fact that he came, that he is here and that he will come again. That doesn't alter the fact that to all those who believe in him, he gives the right to become children of God. Actually we are reborn. And this rebirth does not result from human passion. It is not a physical birth but a spiritual birth. We move from flat, uninspiring, imprisoning, two-dimensional living into a three-dimensional world of glorious technicolour! We move into a place where everything becomes possible because this rebirth comes from God. And all this happens because the Word became a human being and lived here on earth among us. That's the mystery, that's the wonder, that's the indescribable gift that causes our spirits to stand on tiptoe each year when we celebrate the season of Advent. This does not mean that everything becomes easy or that somehow the children of God are protected or shielded from this world's problems and pain. In fact, the reverse is often true. Because we are part of his family, we share a family responsibility and we are not exempt from the highs and lows of living between the times. What makes the difference is that we believe that Jesus, the Word of God made flesh, walks with us and, in a way too mysterious for us to understand, chooses us to bear witness to the light that no darkness can ever master. He invites us to work lovingly with him so that others will be given hope and healing and will know themselves welcomed into the family also.

So where did this all begin? On one level, it has its origins before time began, lovingly held in the heart of God before anything came to be. On another level, we find the clue in a little phrase tucked away in the first chapter of St Luke's gospel. After much investigation, Luke is writing to a friend what he calls a careful summary of all the accounts about the events concerning the birth, life, death and resurrection of Jesus. He is doing this to reassure his friend of the truth of all he had been taught. As we turn the pages of this remarkable and inclusive document, we too can be reassured. What catches my attention and keeps me riveted is the simple phrase, 'It all begins with a Jewish priest, Zechariah' (Lk 1:5). Just imagine going down in history as the person (or persons – for it needed Elizabeth as well!) with whom it all began. At the point where they appear in Luke's narrative they are very old. They had longed for children but had never had any. Something, however, was about to happen for them of an incredible nature. One day when Zechariah was performing his priestly duty in the Temple sanctuary, an angel, a messenger of God, appeared to him and told him that his prayers had been answered, that he and Elizabeth would have a son. This son would be a man with the spirit and power of Elijah, the great prophet of old. He would precede the coming of the Lord, preparing the people for his arrival. God's great plan of redemption for the world was not just an overnight thought or a quick fix. His plans were laid beyond space and time, yet entered space and time in order to be fulfilled. This was the time and Elizabeth and Zechariah were people of destiny, as was their promised son. Zechariah found it humanly impossible to grasp. He needed time to absorb all that he had heard. Time was given. For the whole nine months of Elizabeth's pregnancy he was not able to utter a single word and, when he did speak, the first words were to name his little son John, just as the angel Gabriel had dictated. Then the Holy Spirit came upon him and Zechariah proclaimed this marvellous prophecy that we have come to know, love and revere as the Benedictus. From beginning to end this is a song of hope. Past, present and future are all gathered up in these wonderful words. Throughout the centuries, between then and now, not a day has passed without these words being chanted, sung or spoken by communities of the faithful everywhere. They are more than mere words. Whenever we repeat them in an atmosphere of prayer, I believe they are empowered by the Spirit to have a similar effect upon us as they had upon those who listened to them for the first time long ago. They pierce our darkness with a beam of light, our hearts are lifted and our trust that God's promises to us will be fulfilled, is strengthened.

Zechariah's hope was kept alive by his looking back to tomorrow: when he recalled the faithfulness of God in the past and the promises he had made, he knew that God could not be false to him either today or tomorrow. He would have reflected on how, right throughout the ages from the time of the sacred covenant with their father in the faith, Abraham, God had kept his word to his people. God, in his mercy, would send them a mighty Saviour from the royal line of David just as he had promised through his prophets centuries before. And as he looked at the tiny baby lying in Elizabeth's arms, Zechariah knew that everything Gabriel had told him was true. This baby would grow into such a man as Israel had never experienced, even in the days of Elijah. Zechariah would not live to see it, but in that moment he could see in the Spirit. His son would prepare the way for the Saviour. He would tell the people how to find salvation through forgiveness of their sins. He would be so nurtured in the faith that he would be single-minded in his devotion to God and in his fearless proclamation of the one who was to come after him. He was the great preparer. What was so remarkable about him was that he never sought to be anything else. He fulfilled perfectly the God-given vocation for his life. He repeatedly said to those who questioned him, 'No! I am not the Messiah. But there is one coming who is far greater than I am for he existed long before I did'. Those words can thrill us even today. They certainly did that for those who flocked around John and, as they listened to him, they responded with a resurgence of expectancy and faith. The one who was in existence from before the creation of the world was even now among them although they did not know him. John, by faith, knew he was there somewhere in the crowds. When the time was right, he would appear and he, John, would disappear, his job done, his mission accomplished. John was not being falsely modest. He knew who he was. He knew what he had been called to do, and God had chosen his person well. He did not seek glory for himself. Personal feelings, making a name for himself, had no place in the life of this fearless prophet. John is the Advent figure par excellence: stern, passionate, zealous, but all stemming from an overwhelming love for God and a total desire that all might believe. His was no airy-fairy message, rather, 'Repent and then do the things that prove you have repented. If you have two coats, give one to the poor. If you have food, share it with those who are hungry. Show your honesty. Don't extort money and don't accuse people of things they didn't do. Be content with your pay'. Because of John's testimony, many people moved from a second-hand religion to a living faith. Because of his testimony, what they professed was not just the faith of their fathers, it was their faith, living and vibrant, full of expectancy for the one who was coming. John prepared them. He gave them a spirituality for between the times.

I like to think that, in the mercy of God, Elizabeth and Zechariah were kept from seeing what their son's end would be, that they were left simply to rejoice in this awesome gift and responsibility that now was theirs. On that day, Zechariah knew and, in knowing, spoke it out for all to hear, that the light from heaven was about to break upon his people, that after so many long years of darkness, hope was now shining with a brightness no darkness would ever be able to extinguish and that for them, and all who would ever believe, the path of peace would open up with the Son of God as their guide.

When we look at the times in which we live and at today's world, we could describe them as death-oriented rather than life-giving. So many individuals, communities and nations are walking in the shadow of death. Like the people of old, we have longed for a prophetic voice, for those with a fearless stance who will speak out courageously and with hope for all the forgotten, for the marginalised, for those who feel betrayed and abandoned and for ourselves when we feel lost and overwhelmed. We have longed for a just and peaceful society here in these islands, one free from violence, prejudice, corruption and racism. While we catch glimpses of a different way of living in unexpected places and people, we can so easily slip back, and therefore our hope is fragile. Perhaps it is fragile because we have placed it in human beings, in particular our political and religious leaders, who have feet of clay – as have we all – and in institutions that are far from perfect, including the Church.

There is perhaps no greater calling than to prepare the way for God to come – into people's lives, into communities, into institutions of government, into business and commerce, into churches. How do we do that, we who feel so small and powerless in the face of so much that would compromise, distort, deceive and be defensive? How do we tell people about light in a country that has had religion – words rather than the Word – pushed down its throat for generations, so that people have lost any sense of the reality of the presence of the living Word in their midst and have no conception that light is shining for them? How can belief be awakened again so that we are on tiptoe to welcome the Son of God? What is our testimony? Would others encountering us be pointed beyond us to the Lamb of God and believe, not in us, not in an institution, but in the one who takes away the sin of the world? How do we do that? I think we do it, not so much through our words as through the way we live, through the attitudes we present, through the fruits of the Spirit in our lives. I think we do it through the little daily acts of loving kindness that flow from the heart of a person who knows that they are loved by God. I think we are able to do it when we discover who we are and, in that discovery, realise that nothing will cause us to waver from bearing witness to the light. Who are we? Nothing less than beloved daughters and sons of God, who has called us, as he called John, out of darkness into light. When we appropriate that knowledge deep within our being, then a true humility grows within us. We give up our agenda and pick up God's agenda. And, almost without being aware that it is happening, we will have discovered a spirituality for between the times. Our heart's desire will be that he increases and we decrease. That's a hard one! It led John first to the wilderness, then to a prison cell and execution. But Jesus said of him, 'Of all the people who have ever lived, there is no one greater than John the Baptist'. What a testimony for the one who prepared the way for him to come!

With all the preparation, it seems strange that so many did not recognise the Promised One when he came. We could think it equally strange that, after two thousand years, so many still do not recognise him when he comes. He has not absented himself from his world, nor will he until the appointed time, known only to the Father, but people will not easily see him without our testimony. Words penned by an unknown author in the sixteenth century hold true for us today:

> Thou shalt know him when he comes
> Not by any din of drums,
> Nor the vantage of his airs,
> Nor by anything he wears,
> Neither by his crown,
> Nor by his gown,

For his presence known shall be
By the holy harmony
That his coming makes in me.

That's the key! That's what we long for in ourselves and what he longs for in us. That is our deep and secret yearning. It is actually top of our Christmas list, yet many are scared to put it there in case of disappointment. A holy harmony within, a beloved community in our inner beings that reflects the community, the harmony of the Trinity, Father, Son and Holy Spirit, that was there before the beginning of time. We know that we won't reach that perfect, holy harmony this side of death, but we can, at least, experience glimpses of it. If we are a pilgrim people and an Advent people who are passionately waiting for God to come again and again into our lives and into the life of the world he loves and died to save, then, as each Advent comes around, others should recognise a little bit more of him in us than they did the year before. This is not a cause for anxiety but rather for celebration. We are in the process of becoming 'God's holy people'. It doesn't happen overnight but, with each revelation, rejoicing increases. It is very striking that, out of all the virtues St John could have attributed to Jesus in the prologue to his gospel, the two he singles out are unfailing love and faithfulness. Now, if these are his essential attributes, then we do not need to be fearful about meeting his expectations, nor do we need to be anxious about letting him down. His attitude towards us is always that of unfailing love and faithfulness – always – or else it is not there at all. Unfailing love means love that never fails and faithfulness means full of faith. The Advent Word that God spoke which brought the created order into existence, the Advent Word that he spoke in Jesus when he became a human being, and the Advent Word that he will speak when the time is right for all things to be brought to their fulfilment are irrevocably laced through with unfailing love and faithfulness. That is why Advent is the season of hope. That is the reason behind the celebration. That is what enables us, at times, to live joyfully. And because God is choosing us now, because now is all we have, this is our Advent. And, incredible as it may seem, there is a sense, in this eternal now, that 'it all begins' with us. The time has come.

CHAPTER SEVEN

Between Nazareth and Calvary

'I love you!' – three little words that can bridge the difference between despair and hope, between rejection and acceptance, between isolation and community, between powerlessness and empowerment, between war and peace; three little words that have the power to effect change and, indeed, to alter the course of history. Jesus is God's 'I love you' to the world. His whole mission statement could be summed up in those three words. In fact, in himself, he is the mission statement. Everything that he says and does, as recorded in the gospels, is simply an elaboration, a living out of that declaration. We know practically nothing about his years of growing and working in the village community of Nazareth. Most of Jesus' life is spent there from the time the family returns from exile in Egypt until he begins his public ministry. We hear nothing of him from the age of twelve until he suddenly, at the age of thirty, appears on the public stage. But quietly there must have been a lot happening. St Luke, in a very evocative little statement, says, 'So Jesus grew both in height and in wisdom and he was loved by God and by all who knew him' (Lk 2:52). The rest is cloaked in silence. He would have been nurtured in love, in right relationships and in the faith that was so central to the lives of his earthly parents. He would have known the laughter and innocence of childhood, the awareness of a life beyond the security of family that comes with adolescence, the hard work and struggle to make a living in a poverty-stricken village that had never received a positive press! He would have experienced the harshness of the occupying forces of Rome, but knew also the petty squabbles, the jealousies, dislikes and heartaches as well as the times of joy and celebration that were woven into the fabric of life in Nazareth. His love for the scriptures and the centrality of prayer (prayer being for him an expression of a love relationship with God), he would have seen modelled in his home and given a more formal expression in synagogue. This little, faithful, ordinary life continues until one day, as St Mark very simply puts it, 'Jesus came from Nazareth in Galilee, and he was baptised by John in the Jordan River'.

'You are my beloved son and I am fully pleased with you' (Mk 1:11). Immediately after his baptism by John, Jesus receives this wonderful affirmation of who he is and of God's delight in him. What a high moment! He is thirty years of age, beginning his public ministry after the hidden years of preparation and, right at the start, there is this seal of God's approval. 'Beloved' is an old and very special word. It is not just a descriptive and powerfully affirmative yet gentle word, it is also a command: 'Be loved!' It is a challenge to be vulnerable, to open ourselves up, to let down some of the defensive walls we have built in order to protect ourselves from being hurt, to risk the possibility of being wounded again and to dare to believe that love is there – even for us. At one stage in my life, I went through a particularly dark and difficult time. There did not seem to be any way out. There was no guiding light. I felt abandoned, stripped of everything that had made life worth living. Self-confidence was shattered and trust didn't even feature on my radar screen! At some point, very gradually, I began to emerge from the nightmare, walking now as opposed to crawling inch by painful inch. The particular circumstances are no longer important, but, in retrospect, what helped me along on the next vital stage towards a new beginning, hope and restoration was that someone spoke that word to me: 'Beloved'. It was not only given as a gentle assurance and affirmation, a healing balm; it was given also as an invitation or command, almost a vocation. The challenge was whether or not I would pick up such a calling. What was decisive for me was that the person who uttered the word knew what they were saying, because they had experienced its full meaning in the depths of their own being and so could authentically pass it on, as an image-bearer of Jesus. The heartbeat of a spirituality for between the times is that I, that we, accept the 'I love you' of God in Jesus, that we believe that we are loved and that we continually open ourselves up to this unconditional yet transforming love of God in our lives. It is out of that core that love will flow to others as we also become his image-bearers.

How much Jesus would have to hold on to that affirmation (and challenge) from God in the next three years! In fact, he needs it immediately, for as soon as he is baptised he experiences the wilderness, the time of hard testing. From there he returns in the power of the Spirit and from that point onwards, three short years, everything he does is news. Some hang eagerly on every word, their hearts filled with hope that, after centuries of waiting, this man could be the answer to their prayers, their dreams, their aspirations. Others take note of every word and action for a more sinister reason. They are seeking to build up a case against him in order to have him silenced. He poses a threat to the status quo. He cannot be allowed to upset the delicate balance of power by giving ordinary people ideas about themselves beyond their station in life. He could cause a revolution that would rob them of the relatively comfortable niche they have carved out for themselves, upset local rulers and bring the full wrath of their Roman overlords down upon them. The remarkable thing is that no one is able to ignore him. Everyone has a reaction to him. Some want him for what they think he can do for them – healing, bread, political freedom, miracles of every kind. There are fewer who want him for himself, for who he is. But there *are* some, and for them it is a journey, as they very gradually begin to recognise that here is someone so extraordinary he could only be sent by God. Some are jealous of his influence on the people, and therefore antagonistic to his ministry, others are afraid of the radical things he says and the radical way he lives. There are some in authority who are attracted by his message, but dare not declare it publicly so they meet him in secret. And then there are those who have the awesome, perhaps questionable, privilege of being called by him to be part of an inner group of followers, whom he will train to be bearers of the message also.

Throughout the next three years, Jesus proclaims this good news in many different ways, but the core message is the same. Frequently it is met with rejection. According to St Luke, the first place he announces it is in his home village of Nazareth, in the local synagogue on the Sabbath. He is handed the scroll to read the scriptures and he reads from the prophet Isaiah.

> The Spirit of the Lord is upon me, for he has appointed me to preach Good News to the poor. He has sent me to proclaim that captives will be released, that the blind will see, that the downtrodden will be freed from their oppressors and that the time of the Lord's favour has come.
> (Lk 4:18-19)

And then he says, 'Today, here, in your presence, this prophecy has come true'. At first his hearers are impressed, but not for long. They think they know him. They have him boxed and labelled as the carpenter's son who has done rather well for himself as an itinerant rabbi. But when he makes the claim that God's blessings will flow more readily to outsiders and foreigners than to the chosen people, they are outraged, throw him out and seek to kill him. 'No prophet is accepted in his own home town' (Lk 4:24). The mission statement, embodied in the words of Isaiah and in the person of Jesus, is rejected. They cannot 'see' him or 'hear' him, because their minds are closed. The possibility of him being anything more than the son of Joseph would never even enter their heads.

As we walk along the road between the times, it is conceivable that we, too, miss much because we think we already know. We think we know Jesus. We have him boxed and labelled. We make dogmatic statements about him, seeking to tie him up in our own rules and regulations, and then something happens, and we realise that perhaps we don't know him at all. Another way of putting this would be that we have no trouble dealing with the Jesus we know, but what do we do with the Jesus we don't yet know? We can never say we know another person fully. To do so is somehow to label them as less than human. It is to say that there is nothing more to discover about them, that there's no more mystery. How much more is that true of Jesus! If we feel we've got him 'sussed', then perhaps we have hardly even started on this journey of growing in a love relationship with him, which we affirm is central to our lives. Whatever stage of the journey we're at, there is always more to discover about him. Part of him, maybe the greater part, is still the 'stranger'. He doesn't reveal 'all' in one meeting or even in a lifetime of encounters. We know and believe that his essential nature is love, a love so deep, vast and intimate that, even with all our understanding, we will never be able to grasp it fully. But love can lead us to unfamiliar places, to different ways of seeing, to uncomfortable insights, to risking the loss of things and people we have held dear. It can challenge our comfort zone, disturb our peace, widen our horizons and sometimes take us where we don't want to go. We're happy enough to welcome into our lives the Jesus we've grown up with, the Jesus we know, but how do we cope with this stranger, the Jesus still to be revealed, the one who makes himself little and vulnerable when we think he should be showing his power and authority, the one who is silent when we think he should be shouting from the rooftops, the one who, when we seek to mould him in our image and likeness, shocks us again and again by his diversity?

The Kingdom of God is a difficult concept to put into words. In the end it is mystery. It exists beyond time and yet is rooted within time and space. It is past, present and future. At the beginning of Jesus' public ministry he announced, 'At last the time has come. The Kingdom of God is near. Turn from your sins and believe this Good News' (Mk 1:15). One of the meanings of repentance is to see things differently. This is spelled out most clearly in the Beatitudes, which are the charter for the Kingdom. Jesus is saying, 'Let this be your attitude'. He then goes on to say some rather disturbing things that cause us to question how we can truly live the upside-down nature of his Kingdom, where a lot of what we hold dear is turned on its head? It's a place where we are told to forgive those who wrong us, to go the extra mile, to seek unity, to work for peace, to hunger for justice, to comfort those who mourn, to cultivate a spirit of humility and to be pure in heart! In his person, Jesus embodied the Kingdom fully. But he also said, 'The Kingdom of Heaven is within you'. As we get into the right space with him, as we allow our spirituality to be nurtured, as we embody in our beings the characteristics of the Kingdom, which are love, joy, peace, patience, kindness, goodness, faithfulness, gentleness and self-control, then we are already its citizens. But, obviously, it has still to come in its fullness, so we need to be praying, not with impatience but with passion for his Kingdom to be established fully here on earth. Maybe this is not even our driving ambition anymore, so weary are we, so scarred by the wounds of the journey we have made, so confused are we by this Jesus who keeps beckoning us on and inviting us to go out farther where it is deeper, farther in our picking up the mantle of humility and servant leadership, farther along the reconciliation road, farther along the road to unity, which is our chief evangelistic tool so that the world would believe, deeper in recognising and availing ourselves of the power that is ours for the claiming, in order that an orphaned, weary and anguished world might be restored. Overcome by the pressures, the ordinariness, the busyness, the tiredness and the disillusionment that many feel, it is easy to miss the signs and the opportunities. The key lies in going back to the roots, the core of the message.

On his final journey to Jerusalem Jesus encounters many people, all wanting something. The nearer he gets to the city the darker becomes the cloud of what lies ahead. Yet we don't really get a hint of that. He lives the moment. He is totally present, both to God and to his disciples and those he encounters along the way. Even during the final week of his life, he continues teaching, dialoguing, sharing himself and the truth he embodies in his person. There are recorded moments here that are priceless gems for us on our own pilgrimage. One man, for example, listening to what was going on and, realising that here is no ordinary teacher, gets beyond the religious and political intrigues. He wants to hear more and so he asks Jesus the question, 'Of all the commandments, which is the most important?' Jesus responds in a way that cannot be faulted. He begins with the Shema: 'Hear, O Israel! The Lord your God is the one and only Lord' (Mk 12:29). These words underlie the belief at the very heart of Judaism, that there is only one God. And then he goes on to link the love for God with love for our neighbour, indicating that this sums up the whole message delivered through the law and by the prophets.

The teacher of religious law who has asked the question endorses fully what Jesus has declared. And Jesus is deeply moved by his response. In the midst of the gathering clouds of suspicion and denunciation, in the knowledge that some of the very people listening to him in that crowd would be instrumental in his death and that even his closest friends would desert him, here is one man whose understanding sets him apart. He is grasping what is being said, not only with his head but also with his heart. Jesus says to him, 'You are not far from the Kingdom'. This man is on pilgrimage and Jesus recognises it. He cannot be the same again after this encounter.

What is it that will bring us to the borders of God's Kingdom and enable us to cross over and to journey on with a new identity? It is when we come to the moment of recognition that these two inseparable commandments contain all we need to know in order to live life in all its fullness between the times. 'Hear, each individual who professes faith, hear O Christian Church in Ireland, with all your differences and divisions, hear O Church of Jesus Christ in all the world, the Lord our God is one! And you shall love the Lord your God with all your heart, all your soul, all your mind, all your strength and you shall love your neighbour as yourself.' Jesus lived both these commandments to the full. For him they were inextricably linked, the vertical and the horizontal, and for him they resulted in the cross. For those who choose to identify with him, they may also involve a cross. Perhaps that is one reason why we shy away, why we are individually and collectively cautious and fearful. Perhaps our problem is not that we do not love God – we do, but it is partial. We haven't yet fully surrendered to the love he offers. The other difficulty is that we find it hard to love ourselves. That is then reflected in the way we treat our neighbour. The more difficulty we have in relating in a loving way, either to those close to us or to the stranger, tells us something about our lack of Christ-like care for ourselves, that care that shows mercy, compassion and unconditional love, but also that challenges and brings to our attention some uncomfortable truths. Perhaps it is not until we come to the knowledge that we ourselves are loved by God just as we are, that we will have the freedom to love in return. St John says at one point, 'We love because he loved us first'. Once we experience that love, then we begin to know who we are in him. We are able, in turn, to express that love towards ourselves and others. We are not threatened or defensive, but out of the blessed assurance of God's love for us and ours for him, we are able to continue along the road between the times with a renewed confidence and a trusting heart.

One of the deepest hurts in life is to love someone with every fibre of your being and to have that love spurned, to give your heart to someone and to have that heart broken over and over again. This is the experience of Jesus as he grieves over Jerusalem, the beloved city, and, metaphorically, over a beloved world. He has just made a very courageous statement about who might have a place in the Kingdom and who might not. This would have been anathema to those who heard it, those who believed that they alone were the chosen ones. It could carry with it the charge of treason. The Pharisees were not all bad: many of them were good and godly people. Some come to warn Jesus that, if he persists in talking like this, his life will be in great danger. Herod Antipas is already seeking to kill him. Their advice is that he should leave the region. Jesus, aware of what lies ahead for him, also knows that the time is not quite yet. This gives him enormous freedom to keep on. Herod Antipas is small fry compared to what he is going to face. Then his thoughts go to Jerusalem, and all we can do is stand in awe as we hear this cry from the very depths of the broken heart of God: 'O Jerusalem, Jerusalem, the city that kills the prophets and stones God's messengers! How often I have wanted to gather your children together as a hen protects her chicks beneath her wings, but you would not let me. And now look, your house is left to you empty' (Lk 13:34).

Stepping into the third dimension, what we are hearing here is not just a lament over the Jerusalem of AD 33, but the realisation that over a broken, divided, power-seeking, violent world, God still weeps. He weeps for the hardness of heart that will not soften or listen. He weeps for the forgotten ones, the despairing ones, the sick and the dying ones, the lost and the lonely ones, the impoverished and hopeless ones. He weeps for the few who are rich and greedy, who lust for more and more. He weeps for the silent majority in so many places whose refusal to speak out legitimises terror and torture. He weeps for the wounds growing daily more visible on the whole created order. He weeps for the children. He weeps because he came and comes to give people a name and a sense of identity and belonging. He comes to claim them in love but the wilderness world resists and does not hear or respond to the words and actions of a God whose love does not force itself, but simply offers.

'You wouldn't let me' are perhaps some of the saddest words spoken by Jesus in the gospel narratives. How many times since then have those who have chosen to follow his way and be prophetic voices, image-bearers of his love, heralds of justice and righteousness and his desire for unity in diversity been removed from the face of the earth, assassinated, wiped out because their truth was too uncomfortable, too threatening for the powers of the world to hear! So what happens to the children? What happens to you and me, to our children and grandchildren, to generations yet unborn? Is our house to be left to us empty? In spite of all the wonderful technological advances, all the scientific discoveries, are we, too, going to be left empty – empty of any moral values, empty of meaning, empty of peace, empty of any real happiness, empty of life? Or is there, even yet, a way out of the devastation we have created in this world? I believe there is. Our hope lies in the fact of a God who still allows his heart to be broken over this world, a God who still weeps, a God who does not remove himself from the devastation, but is right there in the midst of the suffering, the dying, the anguish. Here we will find him, in the strangest of ways and in the most unexpected of places, as we choose to walk the little, humble, vulnerable way of Jesus. Our hope lies in a God who can still weep while so many on this world's stage have forgotten how. He weeps because he loves and will not let us go. That's the promise, and while we live in this in-between time that so often seems to be the place of madness, we can even do so sometimes with hope, with love and with joy, because God still loves the world so much that he gives and gives and gives us – Jesus.

Our hope lies also in our response, our picking up the invitation to love and be loved. Pedro Arrupe gets to the essence of it when he says: 'Nothing is more practical than finding God, that is, than falling in love in a quite absolute and final way. What you are in love with, what seizes your imagination will affect everything. It will decide what will get you out of bed in the morning, what you will do with your evening, how you will spend your week-ends, what you read, who you know, what breaks your heart and what amazes you with joy and gratitude. Fall in love, stay in love and it will dictate everything.'[1]

Note

1   Attributed to Pedro Arrupe, SJ, 1907–1991 (Superior General of the Society of Jesus, 1961–1984).

CHAPTER EIGHT

Goodbye and Hello

As we walk along the road between the times, our lives are punctuated by many goodbyes. We leave the security of the womb and, all too soon, bid farewell to childhood innocence. Adolescence soon gives way to adulthood, with its accompanying responsibilities. Almost before we realise it, the busy schedule of our middle years is over and we enter the period of old age, where we know that the next big goodbye will be that of death – others' and our own. Within this overall scenario, there will be other goodbyes of all sorts, different 'letting go' experiences. Some will be much harder to deal with than others for any one of a hundred reasons. The time we have between our birth and our death, be it long or short, is the only time we have been given. Perhaps one of the tests of the quality of our spirituality is how we handle our goodbyes. The word itself carries with it, at very least, a hint of sadness, more often a sense of missing someone or something, and in certain defining moments, a huge sense of sorrow and loss. Goodbyes, however, are necessary for the journey. They create space for other things to emerge. Without them, there can be no new 'hellos', with all that they bring in terms of opportunities for stretching and growth, widening of horizons, building of relationships and deepening understanding.

In the days leading up to his death, Jesus sought, in various ways, to prepare his disciples for his departure. He had spoken to them often during the three years of the kind of death he would die, but their minds could not take on board the thought that the

Messiah would be killed; they were probably largely in denial right up to the crucifixion. On their last evening together, he shared many things with them that they would only really take on board at a later date. At one point, he says very directly that he is leaving. 'But now I am going away to the one who sent me, and none of you has asked me where I am going. Instead you are very sad. But it is actually best for you that I go away, because if I don't, the Counsellor won't come. If I do go away, he will come because I will send him to you' (Jn 16:5-7). Jesus, more than any other, knew how to handle goodbyes. In this leave-taking, he wanted not just to tell them but to show them just how much he loved them. The scene is set in the upper room as the disciples are gathered together for the last time before his death. They don't yet know it, but before another day has passed, he will be dead. St John tells us that Jesus knew that his hour had come to leave this world and return to his Father. Prior to sharing the Passover meal together, he gets up from the table, takes off his outer robe, wraps a towel around his waist, takes a basin of water and begins to wash his disciples' feet. They are all shocked. Once again Jesus has turned their little securities of how things should be upside down. This is no job for the Master! Rather it belongs to the lowest slave. They're all too stunned to speak, all, that is, except Peter who asks 'Why?' – Jesus' action has blown his mind. This is not the way it should be! Peter is on a steep learning curve in relation to what leadership is all about, and what the servant community is all about. He probably doesn't grasp the full significance of what is happening then and there. That understanding would come after years of reflecting and growing on his spiritual journey, but, nonetheless, this is an important moment of recognition for him. His initial reaction is, 'You will never wash my feet'. Jesus responds immediately in what seems to be a very harsh way: 'If I don't, you won't belong to me. You will have no place with me.'

Peter thought he had understood, but perhaps in this moment realises that he has hardly even begun to understand. He would much rather have done something for Jesus than receive this act of love and service from him. Most of us would sympathise with Peter. We can be much happier when we're giving than when we're receiving. When we're giving we can usually remain in control of the situation. We don't have to be vulnerable or show any sign of weakness. But when we receive we are, in essence, saying that we haven't got it all together, that we have needs and fragilities, that in ourselves we are not whole and that there is something within us that actually needs what the other person is offering. Peter wasn't very used to touch, to tenderness, to gentleness. It disarmed him. He didn't know what to do with it. In fact, they were probably all disarmed. This would have been the last time before his death that Jesus would have had intimate contact with the twelve. As he moved from one to the other, washing their feet, it was as if he were saying to each one a silent goodbye. Certainly, it was an act of love for these twelve people who had shared so much with him. St John says, 'He now showed the disciples the full extent of his love' (Jn 13:1b). Is it not rather strange that, if this is a demonstration of the full extent of Jesus' love for humankind, we in the Christian Church have pushed it to the edges and only perform a sanitised version of it once a year on Holy Thursday? St John's gospel is the only one that has no account of the Last Supper. Instead, he movingly recounts this awesome action. In a way, it is also a sacrament. It is not so much the particular action as the mind-blowing image it represents. This washing of the feet was a powerful icon for the disciples. It is Jesus, as part of his farewell, showing them a new model of leadership, seeking to reveal to them who he is, to let them in on the essence of his being, that he, to whom the Father had given everything, who had come from God and was going back to God, chooses to exercise his leadership through the power of love. He becomes vulnerable before them. Then he says to them that this is the sort of leadership they should offer also. 'You call me "Teacher" and "Lord" and you are right because it is true. And since I, the Lord and Teacher have washed your feet, you ought to wash each other's feet. I have given you an example to follow. Do as I have done to you' (Jn 13:13b-15). And then he adds, 'Do this and you will be blessed'. There are more Beatitudes in the gospels than those we find in Matthew chapter 5 or Luke chapter 6, and this is one of them.

When we feel vulnerable the instinct is to self-protect. The way we do that is to seek to control situations and other people. There is something quite frightening about simply being open and transparent (which is not to be confused with naivety or having no boundaries). It is something to do with knowing oneself and being aware of one's relationship with God, so that we are not primarily swayed by what other people think of us, or about being manipulated if we show a side that others might interpret as weakness. It is a sign of spiritual and emotional maturity, a state that Peter had not yet achieved, and one that probably takes each of us a lifetime to reach, if we ever do. Christian leadership is modelled for us by the Servant King, who willingly becomes lower than everyone else in order that he might raise them up into a knowledge of who they really are, beloved daughters and sons of God. Putting such an understanding into action is a journey, a vital one for between the times. And the road we travel has a name. It is the path of blessing.

The washing of the disciples' feet is the beginning of Jesus' final descent into littleness, into total vulnerability and brokenness, into death. It is the start of his final emptying of himself, in order that we might be full, that we might live. Goodbye really means 'God be with you'. As he bids farewell in this way to his friends, Jesus is seeking to convey the message, 'May God, the God you have seen mirrored in me, the God who is full of unfailing love and faithfulness be with you through all you are going to experience up ahead'. Jesus' goodbye at Calvary is a slow, merciless agony, where he himself experiences utter abandonment and yet, in a supreme act of trust, still commits his spirit into the Father's keeping. It is his passion for God and his resulting compassion for others that keep him nailed to the cross through all this anguished letting-go, until it is accomplished. His goodbye, his 'God be with you' from the cross embraces a dying thief who is promised a place in Paradise, his mother whom he commits to the care of his close friend, and all of humankind whose actions put him there and for whom he prays forgiveness. Only then do we hear the shout of victory, 'It is finished!'

It is finished and, at the same time, only just beginning. The disciples are not aware of it yet, but this goodbye is the prelude to another hello. For the moment they are hiding, huddled together in fear, grief, confusion, guilt and shame. Their hopes and dreams have ended up on the scrapheap outside the city, where he has been crucified. If or when they talk, it merely results in an endless cycle of recriminations and 'if onlys' that get them nowhere, so, after a while, two of them leave to return to their home village of Emmaus about seven miles away. These two, their thoughts, words and body language spelling hopelessness, fear and defeat, are not aware of anything but the misery they have left in that upper room and the nothingness into which they feel they are walking. Everything that has given life meaning over the last few years has been stripped away from them. All they can think of is that Jesus has gone. He is dead. It is beyond their powers of comprehension to take on board the concept of resurrection, of which some of the women among their number have spoken. A stranger joins them on the road and asks what is troubling them. They do not recognise him either by a greeting or a glance. They tell their story of the last few days, their dashed hopes, their broken dreams and the confusion caused by reports of sightings of Jesus alive. It is at this point that the stranger begins to enable them to reflect on what has happened in a different way, to be aware. There is more 'unlearning' done in these short seven miles than probably at any other point in history. They begin to be totally engaged with what this stranger is saying. In place of cold despair, a steadily increasing warmth invades their hearts. They are filled with new insight and gratitude, so much so that they insist, as they reach their destination, that the stranger come in and dine with them. Within a few minutes a full awareness bursts upon them. They have been awakened to a new understanding of the scriptures. As they see the familiar action of the breaking of the bread and as they hear the beloved voice giving thanks to God, they know the truth of resurrection. Goodbye has been transformed into hello. Even though he disappears, their burning desire is to make known this amazing news. Jesus risen has changed everything. It causes them to run back with winged feet to the place which, a few hours earlier, they had left in such dejection and fear. Their new awareness, held within a redemptive remembering, enables them to recognise that God is choosing them now and now and now. Their thoughts of the past are transformed. They are now looking back to tomorrow. Their journey back to Jerusalem is like a bridge between the times.

Traditionally, the day between Good Friday and Easter Sunday is called Holy Saturday. For many of us there is little joy in the day. As it was for the disciples, so it tends to be for us; it is cloaked in the greyness of loss or purposelessness. In the Catholic and High Anglican traditions however, the joy of Easter bursts forth in the evening with the Vigil Mass. There is something immensely moving and hopeful as the Paschal fire is lit; light once more pierces the darkness and God says 'Hello' again to us in Jesus risen. But the questions remain. Do we, in the Church at large, bear witness to resurrection? Are we an Easter people? Is it possible that others, encountering us, would know that we are the bearers of the greatest good news ever to break into these in-between times? Most of the time it seems as if we, certainly in the western world, present an image of being imprisoned in the flatness, the deadness of Holy Saturday. Tony Campolo wrote a book entitled *It's Friday, But Sunday's Comin'*.[1] Have we that sort of expectancy and vibrancy, or are we still waiting for someone to roll away the stone from the tomb of our dashed hopes, our buried vision, our guilt, our doubts and fears? It can be a very large stone. Where are the messengers of resurrection who will announce to us that he is not here entombed with our broken dreams and limited understanding, but that we will find him out there in Galilee of the nations, there ahead of us, yet still waiting for us to catch up? What will cause the Church to come rushing back to the place of meeting with winged feet because now we know, in a place beyond our heads, that goodbye has been transformed into hello? What will enable us to look back to tomorrow and to be, in ourselves, a bridge between the times? It's been Friday/Saturday too long in our life and witness. I believe that in the midst of all the caution, the humiliation, the guilt, the despair at what seems like a dying of the Church in all its branches, there can even now be heard, for those with ears to hear, the first sounds of a cry that will rise in joyous crescendo as we acknowledge that we are a forgiven and forgiving people: 'It may be Friday, but Sunday's coming!' With that will come the incredibly humbling, yet irresistible awareness that God is choosing us now and now and now.

Of course there is another goodbye. St Luke tells us that Jesus appears many times to his apostles after the crucifixion, proving to them in different ways that he really is alive, and he uses these occasions to talk with them about the Kingdom of God. This particular in-between time lasts for only forty days. The moment comes when he is to leave them. The friends of Jesus are commissioned to go into all the world as witnesses to him, as bearers of the good news that there is forgiveness for all those who turn to him. What he has done for them, he will do for others because of their testimony. They are to go, not in their own strength, but in his and they are to go with his authority. Before he says his last goodbye to them in the form they have known him, he gives this final assurance: 'I am with you always, even to the end of time.' It is not 'I have been' nor 'I will be' but 'I am'. In the eternal now that transcends the world of time and space, there is the ever-present reality of Jesus with us. It is not up to us to determine how long the time will be between his ascension into heaven and his final return. 'The Father sets those dates and they are not for you to know,' says Jesus (Acts 1:7).

Part of Jesus' first goodbye before his crucifixion is to offer something to his friends. 'I am leaving you with a gift,' he says, 'peace of mind and heart. And the peace I give isn't like the peace the world gives. So don't be troubled or afraid' (Jn 14:27). Peace is his parting gift, but it is also his hello to them after his resurrection. It seems, therefore, that this is something that he considers very important. It is obviously not something that can be bought or bargained for. It is sheer grace. What is it? It has something to do with freedom from fear. When offered, it is nearly always accompanied by the words, 'Do not be afraid'. In this uncertain world, where there is so much that would cause us to be fearful and anxious, what we yearn for, perhaps more than anything else, is that inner peace, a calm that remains no matter what storms are raging. And yet we allow ourselves to be robbed of it so easily. Peace of mind and heart comes from trusting God, from believing that he has our shalom, our total well-being at heart, no matter how things may seem at times. Peace comes in the person of the Comforter, the Holy Spirit, whom Jesus has promised will never leave us. The gift of peace becomes a reality at Pentecost. The Holy Spirit up till then has been with them but now he will live within them. He is the hello again of Jesus after the goodbye, the 'God be with you' of Ascension. He will lead them into truth. He will teach them, remind them of everything Jesus told them and will reveal to them whatever he receives from Jesus. So the Holy Spirit is the presence and the power of Jesus alive and active in the world today and in the lives of those who believe. For, as well as peace, the other gift is power. 'When the Holy Spirit has come upon you, you will receive power and will tell people about me everywhere' (Acts 1-8a). And that is what they did. At the very end of St Mark's gospel are these words: 'The disciples went everywhere and preached, and the Lord worked with them, confirming what they said by many miraculous signs' (Mk 16:20). They were empowered by the Spirit to do the same things as Jesus had done – and greater. They healed the sick, raised the dead, cast out demons and announced that the Kingdom of Heaven was near. The signs of the Kingdom included all these things, not just the preaching of the word. Isn't it strange that we in the Church have largely confined ourselves to the latter? Proclaiming the word is important and necessary, but people's minds and hearts will be opened much more readily if that word is accompanied by miraculous signs. Perhaps our faith has grown tired. Perhaps our belief systems have lost their expectancy. We say, 'That was then and this is now. We live in a different age. God doesn't operate like that any more'. How do we know? One thing is certain, the authority of Jesus and the power of the Holy Spirit haven't changed or diminished or grown weary.

If we have really experienced the hospitality, the welcome back of God through forgiveness, then we won't be able to stop ourselves from being witnesses, no matter what the cost. The early disciples announced the message of repentance and forgiveness of sins with great power and authority. Everyone could see the transformation in them. They knew that they had been with Jesus not only by the authority of their words but by the miracles they performed and by the love that pervaded everything they did. They were truly a forgiven and forgiving people. They were witnesses to what the power of love and forgiveness can do in someone's life. They literally took this good news to the nations.

Maybe, after so many years, we need to have our minds opened to understand afresh who this Jesus really is, crucified and risen, ascended into heaven, seated at the right hand of the Father, constantly interceding for us, so that we might, in all humility, pick up his mantle of authority and, empowered by the Holy Spirit, begin in our particular 'Jerusalem' to be witnesses to this, the greatest of all good news.

And whenever it all seems too much for us, when we wonder what we're doing on this crazy journey anyway, when that inner peace we crave seems to be a scarce commodity, when the power and authority to witness to this upside-down Kingdom of God appears to have vanished, when we can't see the way ahead, it is good to remember that one of the loveliest names given to the Holy Spirit is the Paraclete, meaning 'the one who answers the cry'. Just as a mother's whole being is attuned to hear the tiniest whimper of her child, so the heart of God, the Holy Spirit, is finely tuned to our beings and he will not fail us. What has seemed like a goodbye is transformed into another hello, as he comes with the assurance that he has called us, he has chosen us and we are his beloved – now and now and now.

Note

1   Tony Campolo, *It's Friday, But Sunday's Comin'* (Berkhamsted, Herts, England: Word (UK) Ltd, 1985).

CHAPTER NINE

Passionately Waiting

Terry Donaghy, a local solicitor, died on the Feast of the Epiphany, 2009, while on a prayer walk in Belfast for Gaza and for peace in the Middle East. He was a member of our Board of Directors in Restoration Ministries and was actively involved in many cross-community and ecumenical ventures. He was a great encourager – that is, he gave courage to the rest of us. Perhaps his biggest yet quiet and relatively hidden contribution to Christian unity was his faithful pilgrimage every week to different churches to share in their worship, while remaining true to his own tradition. Terry would attend the Saturday Vigil Mass and then on Sunday mornings he had a rota of sixteen churches that he visited, including Presbyterian, Methodist, Church of Ireland, Non-Subscribing Presbyterian, Baptist and Brethren. He didn't do it with a trumpet blast but with a quiet, deep humility and with great joy. In his person he embodied the prayer of Jesus 'that they may be one'. We could never measure, nor will we know this side of death, what effect that faithful and repeated action has had in the unseen world, but I know without a shadow of a doubt that the heart of God rejoiced and that blessings have flowed in unexpected places simply because Terry did it, a consequence arising directly from his life of prayer. So, he leaves us with a legacy of hope and hope is perhaps the biggest gift we need at the moment. We give thanks to God for all those who, throughout the long hard years of the Troubles in Northern Ireland, never, ever, gave up, but kept on, passionately praying, working, waiting because of the hope that was in them.

In 2008, Restoration Ministries was twenty years old. When we were first founded, we sensed our calling was to be present especially to those who were on the front line of action, either in church or community, those who might need a listening ear and/or prayer ministry for some of the wounds their vocation to be peacemakers had inflicted upon them. It soon became evident that these were not necessarily the people who would come – for a variety of reasons – but that people from every walk of life and experience began to cross the doors of what is now called Restoration House, many of them, we believe, finding help and a measure of healing. We also quickly recognised that reconciliation was in itself a form of healing and was of vital importance if there was to be any future for us as a community in Northern Ireland and for those who would come after us. Out of that evolving pilgrimage, our work and witness quietly grew. We were still in the midst of the Troubles. Nobody had any idea how long it would take us to arrive at some sort of stability that would grow into the peace that we now have. We began to seek every opportunity we could to bring people together across the divide – we had one division then, now there are many – in a safe place with no hidden agenda other than to build relationships and friendships. One of our core beliefs is that attitudes are about hearts and minds and that hearts and minds are changed through the building of relationship. So, we place a great deal of emphasis on hospitality. If I were asked what is at the heart of the gospel, I would say a restoration of hospitality – hospitality between ourselves and God, hospitality between the alienated parts of our own inner beings, hospitality between ourselves and others, especially those who are different from us, and hospitality between ourselves and the whole created order. In a small and largely hidden way, in all humility, that is the heart of the work that Restoration Ministries seeks to do.

'That all may be one' is a prayer, a calling out to God, a cry of the heart that should be rising from the very depths of all those who profess to be Christian of any tradition, not just in Ireland but around the world. If it is so clearly the passion of Jesus for the Church in all its branches, then it should be our passion too. Again and again in scripture we are reminded that it is right relationships that will prepare the way for God to come afresh into our national and individual lives. The psalmist tells us that where brothers and sisters dwell together in unity, there God commands a blessing. It is an actual divine command, not a suggestion or a wish! How much are we in need of blessing in these days, not only for ourselves and our communities, but for this world that seems to be overshadowed more than ever by the dark clouds of depression, oppression, anxiety, war, injustice and amorality? But perhaps the most pressing reason, and the one which should be irresistible to every follower of Jesus, is that this was the main heartbeat of his prayer on the night before he died, namely that we might be one so that the world would believe. Our demonstration of unity is the chief evangelistic tool that we have been given in order to point people to faith, to Jesus. And yet, for the most part, we ignore it. How can we become in our own beings, in our churches and communities part of the answer to the prayer of Jesus, even at this late date? Perhaps we need to rediscover our passion for praying for what was so obviously the desire of his heart, and after we have passionately waited in prayer, then to follow up with prayer-motivated action, to put our bodies where our words and prayers have been. If we are attuned to listen then we are going to pick up that heartbeat, that desire for community, for unity that is central to the being of God, Father, Son and Holy Spirit and we will want to seek to live that prayer in all we do.

Each year during the Week of Prayer for Christian Unity people from different traditions come together to pray. It is right and good that they do so. But somehow, in Ireland, there was more of a sense of importance and urgency about these annual services and regular social meetings twenty years ago, because we were caught in the midst of strife, mistrust, anger, bitterness and great pain. To come out to a cross-community or interdenominational gathering gave us the feeling that we were doing something, however small, to make a statement that we wanted to be reconciled, that we wanted peace, that we wanted to live in harmony with our sisters and brothers of other religious traditions and cultures and of different political persuasions. There was also, if we're honest, a certain amount of kudos, a certain adrenalin flow that came from associating ourselves with events such as these. That has long since gone. No more glory attached, if there ever was, but simply the hard road of keeping on keeping on, seeking still to have our eyes focused on the goal of unity, harmony and peace – if you like, the goal of reconciliation. But it's much harder to do it today than it was even eleven years ago when we were just embarking on that rather fragile road of relative peace. We are still a violent society with the frightening and awful 'intimacy' of the knife and of drug-related crime, but with the absence of explosions and shootings, and with long-awaited devolution now taking root, people, by and large, have allowed their weariness of all the long years to come to the surface. This presents itself as seeming apathy. Generally the public doesn't consider reconciliation or bridge building to be so much their task as that of their elected representatives. All of this contributes to the seemingly insurmountable wall that blocks the way for those who still have that commitment, that passion burning in their hearts, even though the flame at times is weak and flickering. This is not to say that there aren't many positive things happening. We have come a long way. There are far more interdenominational gatherings and cross-community opportunities on offer than there have ever been, but somehow the energy, the expectancy, the enthusiasm isn't there in the same measure or with the same urgency or intensity as it was a number of years ago. Today, we face not just our familiar and ancient divisions, but the 'discomfort' of welcoming people of every creed, nation and culture, a glorious diversity that, if we do not address it fully, threatens to call up again our fear of difference, our sectarianism, even our racism. It is not that God is calling us to uniformity; that would be terribly boring. In fact, it was God himself who created diversity and saw that it was good. Rather he is calling us to a unity in that very diversity. He's calling us to a deeper and much more committed realisation that we are members of the one family, sisters and brothers in one faith expressed in different ways. We have one Lord, one faith, one baptism and yet, because we equate difference with division and separation, we have not been a voice of hope for the world. Think of all the riches we have missed out on over centuries because we have jealously guarded our own way of doing things and declared it to be the only way. That sort of religious pettiness, accompanied by the perception that we are somehow divorced from the reality of a diverse and multi-faceted society, is what, perhaps more than anything else, has contributed to the drift away from 'Church'. Yet people are still hungry for a spirituality to enable them to truly live between the times. Together, in humility, as a community of wounded healers, we have something to offer them. Separately we do not.

On the Wednesday of Holy Week 2008, my latest little grandniece arrived into this world. I could hardly wait to meet her and the day was set for Good Friday. On Holy Thursday night I had a very vivid dream. In the dream, I arrived to be introduced to her. She refused my advances and said very clearly and distinctly, 'You have a weak and divided heart'. I awoke almost immediately, stunned and shocked. Of course the actual meeting was wonderful and we already have a relationship going! But what was the dream saying? I realise that part of it I need to take personally for my own spiritual journey. On reflection, however, I think that in the dream I was the representative of yesterday's generation, in both church and society, perhaps especially church. The two-day-old scrap of humanity was tomorrow's, in all its promise, expectancy and innocence. The gap between is where we have not been authentic and so have let down today's generation – and tomorrow's. We are in a new century with a new generation of young Irish women and men who remember nothing of the long years of conflict, except what their parents and the rest of us feed them. Therein lies the rub. If we have not dealt with the legacy of the past, what are we handing on to the next generation? Will history repeat itself or will there be a new story because we have had the generosity of spirit to let go, the courage to face some uncomfortable truths and the commitment and passion to keep on believing and building for this new day that we have been given? Can we make known the receipt of the message that has been entrusted to us in a new language for a post-church generation, a language that bears the hallmarks of repentance, that is, that sees things differently; a language of forgiveness, the greatest power in the world and one which we, who are expected to be the experts, haven't even begun to tap into yet or else have sought to force on people before they are ready; and a language that is authenticated by our lives? We need to be looking back to tomorrow together, to remember and to lay down that which has not been helpful, and to pick up only those things that will empower us to be a bridge between the times.

The truth is that we, as the Church, have had a weak and divided heart. For me, the true meaning of remembrance is to put flesh again on the past. How can we remember other events together when we can't even engage in the most precious act of remembrance together, the sacrament of communion, where by faith we put flesh again on the great act of redemption that makes all acknowledging of the past possible? Teillhard de Chardin said that as Christians we are called to stand where the cross is erected. The only bridge that can bring together the divided heart is in the shape of a cross. When we stand where the cross is erected, we cannot have a weak and divided heart. For more than thirty years, the shadow of the cross fell over this small piece of earth that is Northern Ireland, and in its shadow terrible things were done. For those who stood where it was erected and sought to be a bridge, we give thanks to God. Can we, even now, pick up that mantle? I believe that the answer is 'Yes', not because of our past record, but because from that same cross, on this side of Easter, there streams a light that changes everything. In the light of that same cross, we can retell the story in a way that may bring us all to repentance, so that even yet we may sing the Lord's song together in this strange land of new beginnings, because we will have reached an awareness that God is choosing us now and now and now. With the awareness there comes responsibility, not at some future date, but right now. Do we need to lobby our religious leaders, as well as praying for them, to even yet hold a national service of thanksgiving for the favour God has shown to this island, but also of repentance for either what, as Church, we did or failed to do? Do we need to be asking them to declare publicly that the call to unity – not uniformity – is the chief call of God to the Church today in Ireland and elsewhere so that the world would believe? Do we need to be extending the hospitality of our different denominations to one another on a far more regular basis than the Week of Prayer for Christian Unity? Do we as Church members need to take this so seriously that we would do an awful lot before we would refuse such an invitation –

because it comes, ultimately, not from any other human being but from Jesus himself? Do we need to be openly declaring in a far more courageous way than we have done heretofore, by our words and by our actions, that we are truly sisters and brothers in Christ? It may be a simplistic thing to say, but true nonetheless, that we really need each other. Dare we recognise fully that the body of Christ is incomplete without each other, not only Protestants, Catholics, Orthodox and the New Churches, but women and men, old and young? With the influx of our new neighbours from so many different countries, we are being made aware that God is the creator of diversity, that he rejoices in it and sees that it is good. The word 'welcome' comes from the old English 'You are well come'. If we in Ireland have not been able to say that, either to our Protestant or Catholic neighbours, how are we going to be able to extend hospitality to the thousands who, whether we choose to recognise it or not, are changing the face of this island for ever? It is a huge challenge. Our heart's hospitality is being stretched and it seems as if we are resisting. The danger is that when there is resistance to stretching, something may snap. If that were to happen, we could be plunged into something very ugly once again. Even though there has been so much good work done by individuals and by organisations committed to peace building, the powerful negative emotions released by the lie that 'all difference is bad and suspect' have not been fully addressed. We have still an enormous task to do in order that people may be seized by the vision of a beloved community. Where is the unity of hearts, of spirits, of bodies that the world will sit up and take notice of? Do we need to be praying for and expecting the emergence of a new prophetic voice that will challenge us to stand, and to stand together, even at this late date, where the cross is erected? What can we do to speed up the day when we can all share in the sacrament of communion? Can we be brave enough and vulnerable enough and loving enough to frequently attend one another's sacrament of the Eucharist and stand in the pain of not receiving, stand where the cross is erected until Easter truly comes and we can remember together and move forward together and die and live again together? As we acknowledge the past, how sharp is our awareness that God is choosing us now – and now is all we have?

Etty Hillesum, a young Dutch woman, kept diaries during the chaotic time of the early years of World War II. Her own inner journey was a remarkable one, a journey that eventually took her, through her own choice and out of deep compassion for her own people, to the holding camp at Westerbork and to her eventual death in Auschwitz at the age of twenty-nine. At one point she writes: 'In this tempestuous, havoc-ridden world of ours, all real communication comes from the heart. Outwardly we are being torn apart, and the paths to each other lie buried under so much debris that we often fail to find the person we seek. We can only continue to live together in our hearts, and hope that one day we may walk hand in hand again.'[1] For me a very powerful definition of reconciliation is simply 'walking together again'. So why are so many of us afraid of it and why do so many resist it? What would it take for us to walk hand in hand along the road between the times? At another point in her diaries, Etty says, 'O God, times are hard for frail people like myself. I know that a new and kinder day will come. I would so much like to live on, if only to express all the love I carry within me. And there is only one way of preparing the new age, by living it even now in our hearts.'[2] Is it possible for us as individuals and churches to really begin to express all the love we carry within us? As we look back, have we adequately prepared for this new day by living it in our hearts, passionately waiting, praying without ceasing, nurturing the love relationship between ourselves and God? Are we now equipped to seize the moment, so that what the politicians are seeking to do at one level may be underpinned and strengthened at grass-roots level by right relationships, acceptance of difference and a desire for community? What is our destiny as the Church of Jesus Christ? Jesus said, 'I have other sheep, too, that are not in this sheepfold. I must bring them also, and they will listen to my voice, and there will be one flock with one shepherd' (Jn 10:16). That is his dream. That is his vision. Is it ours? I believe with all my heart that if Christians in Ireland moved this to the top of their agenda, Ireland could yet fulfil its God-given destiny to be a sign of hope and encouragement and restored hospitality to the rest of the world. We're not asked to do it on our own, or even to take one giant step that will take us to the place where he wants us to be. The giant step has already been taken. God has already reconciled us to himself through the life, death and resurrection of Jesus. On the cross, God gave himself as the answer to this prayer. Because of that supreme action, we are equipped to be reconcilers, to be hope bearers, encouragers, all contributing to that day when there will be one fold and one shepherd. Some time ago I came across these words. For me, they are passionate words. 'Someone or something may delay your destiny but they cannot kill it off.' They cannot kill it because it does not belong so much to us as to God. It has been tailor-made for us by the God who knows our fragilities, our stubbornness, our weakness as well as our strengths and attractiveness. He will accomplish his purpose.

In September 2008, we caught a glimpse of what could be when ninety Church leaders from different Christian traditions in Ireland met in Dromantine near Newry, Co. Down – bishops and clergy, members of religious orders and lay people. They came together to explore, in the company of Jean Vanier, how we might move forward together in diversity. The defining moment of a grace-filled day came when the entire company looked back to tomorrow and washed each other's feet. The passion and the gentleness of Jesus were translated into this act of humble service to one another. In a very moving and powerful way it united people across many divides. There was a heightened awareness, a sense of the eternal now and that together we were being called and chosen again by the community of the 'I am' who is God, Father, Son and Holy Spirit.

John O'Donohue wrote a blessing for love in a time of conflict. It speaks powerfully to me about restoration, about walking together again.

> When the gentleness between you hardens
> And you fall out of your belonging with each other,
> May the depths you have reached hold you still.
>
> …
>
> Now is the time for one of you to be gracious
> To allow a kindness beyond thought and hurt,
> Reach out with sure hands
> To take the chalice of your love,
> And carry it carefully through this echoless waste
> Until this winter pilgrimage leads you
> Towards the gateway to spring.[3]

We have been through an echoless waste, but now we need each other, not only those of us who live in different parts of this island, but especially all of us in the different branches of the Christian Church. We have always needed each other. Over hundreds of years the 'gentleness between us has hardened' and who can even remember truly when we fell out of belonging with each other. I believe that the depths we have reached can even yet be used in a redemptive way to hold us in that place of hope. Now is the time for us to be gracious. Now is the time to declare that we are living in a new day.

Now is the time to reach out with sure hands to take the chalice of that love that underpins everything, that love that unites us, the love we know in Jesus, and carry it carefully through this fragile time as prisoners of hope. We do so knowing that we are being led towards the gateway to spring, to resurrection, to the fulfilment of our destiny as children of God. We happen to have been born in Ireland and, because of that, can now be bearers of hope to the world. Out of all the debris of the years we can offer a spirituality for between the times.

Notes

1   Etty Hillesum, *An Interrupted Life and Letters From Westerbork* (New York: Henry Holt and Company, Inc., 1996), p. 175.

2   Ibid., p. 185.

3   John O'Donohue, 'For Love in a Time of Conflict', *Benedictus*, p. 50.

CHAPTER TEN

Falls The Shadow

If we are truly in earnest about finding a spirituality for between the times, if we are willing to be seized by such a mode of being, if our prayer is, 'Lord, make me; make me into the person you had in your mind and your heart from the very beginning', then God will honour that desire, even though it may lead us to the place of hard testing. Our hope lies in the fact that the passion of Jesus, the reason he came, was to make us into his new creation. That being the case, we make the statement of faith: 'He will lead us through' and fling it against any shadows that we may confront. It costs a lot to be a bridge, to look back to tomorrow. When I look back through history, apart from Jesus, the figure that stands out for me as one who truly forged a spirituality for between the times was St Francis of Assisi. In the well-known prayer attributed to him we are challenged to live as citizens of another kingdom, the upside-down kingdom of God, to live the exact opposite of what we find in our world. His prayer begins with the plea: 'Lord, make me an instrument of your peace.' It's a very courageous prayer to pray. It's really saying to God that he can have a free hand in our lives. It's requesting that he 'make' us into peacemakers, instruments that he can use to bring his peace to troubled people, to torn relationships, to divided communities, to a war-weary world. It's asking that he make us into a bridge between the times. This is an awesome thing to pray for, and we need to be aware that there will be a cost involved. In order for us to develop, to mature into such, it may be that we, too, have to go through our times of hard testing. It certainly will mean that, whatever it costs, we discover that peace within ourselves, for how can he use us if we haven't got for ourselves what we want to give to others? Really we are praying that we become image-bearers of Jesus, who embodies in himself all those characteristics that bring the peace that the world can neither give nor take away.

St Francis of Assisi lived eight centuries ago, born in 1182. Elizabeth Goudge writes of him: 'His influence upon European music, art, drama and politics has been a study for many scholars, yet it is as a Christian that he matters to us, as a humble poor man who set himself to tread as closely as he could in the footsteps of Christ, perhaps as closely as any man has ever done, and by so doing shames us. Looking at him we see what it means to be Christian, and what it costs. His story is not only endearing, it is terrifying. Yet without the fear and shame he would not have so much power over us, for we know in our hearts that what is worth having costs everything. And so his power lives on and we cannot measure it because it is nowhere near its end.'[1] Whether he actually wrote the prayer 'Lord, make me an instrument of your peace' or not to my mind doesn't really matter. What matters is that it sums up his life and finds more than a passing echo in our hearts. It is probably the best-known and best-loved prayer after the Lord's Prayer, but, like the Lord's Prayer, if we really began to take it seriously, it would challenge us and stretch us more than we think we could cope with. You have only to read a life of St Francis to see what it cost him. You have only to turn to the gospels, to the accounts of the passion, to see what it cost Jesus. Richard Rohr, a Franciscan, writes of his father in the faith, 'Francis is first of all saying that we cannot change the world except insofar as we have changed ourselves. We can only give away who we are. We can only offer to others what God has done in us. We have no real head answers. We must be an answer. We only know the other side of journeys that we have made ourselves. Francis walked to the edge and so he could lead others to what he found there. All the conflicts and contradictions of life must find a resolution in us before we can resolve anything out there. Only the forgiven can forgive, only the healed can heal, only those who stand daily in need of mercy can offer mercy to others.'[2]

> Lord, make me an instrument of your peace.
> Where there is hatred, let me sow love;
> Where there is injury, pardon;
> Where there is doubt, faith;
> Where there is despair, hope;
> Where there is darkness, light;
> Where there is sadness, joy.

St Francis, early on in his pilgrimage of faith, heard God saying to him, 'Francis, rebuild my church, for you can see it is in ruins'. At first, in his youthful enthusiasm, he took this literally, that he was to rebuild the tumbled-down little church of San Damiano, but later he realised that the call was a much deeper one – it was to rebuild the body of Christ. In order to do that, Francis had to allow God to 'make' him. This was a process that went on throughout his whole life. In order for him to be a rebuilder, a maker, he himself had to be restored, to be made. This was his spiritual journey and the reason he was so effective. The only way that he could become an instrument of the peace of God was to continually open himself up to the transforming power of the Holy Spirit at work within him. In his writings we find these words: 'They are truly makers who amidst all they suffer in this world maintain peace in soul and body for the love of our Lord Jesus Christ.'[3] Like his Master before him, the passion that drove him was love, love for God and a resulting love for humanity, especially humanity that had been pushed to the edges, whether that be the edges of poverty, of reason, of disease, of despair, of disillusionment, of anguish or pain. To be 'made' by God cost Francis much, but he walked (or rather he sang and 'danced' his way) along this road with joy, as did Jesus. The writer to the Hebrews, seeking to encourage some of the early believers, says this, 'Let us run with endurance the race that God has set before us. We do this by keeping our eyes on Jesus, on whom our faith depends from start to finish. He was willing to die a shameful death on the cross because of the joy he knew would be his afterward' (Heb 12:1b-2). For us, it might seem impossible. We might make it on our bleeding hands and knees, but to do it with joy?

Perhaps part of the secret lies in the fact that it is not so much change that we are talking about here as transformation. We cling to the familiar, even when it is uncomfortable, because in the familiar we think we find our security. As Christians we affirm with our lips that God is our security, but when the chips are down, the question is often not to whom do we run, but rather where we run to. And usually it is to the old place, whatever that may be – the womb of our particular tradition or culture, the haven of old relationships, the job that has given us an identity or a sense of being safe. Usually we only 'let go', we only move when the old place becomes more uncomfortable, even more unbearable than the thought of being in a wilderness time, a sort of no-man's-land that is almost inevitable as a time of transition before the new place begins to look attractive.

For us to be instruments of God's peace, we, too, need to be made. We need to be 'rebuilt' in order that we may be makers. It is a time of refining, or defining, of reflection, of restoration. It is a time of transformation, of movement. Before there is movement on the outside, there needs to be movement or transformation on the inside. This prayer brings opposites together. Within all of us there is a shadow side and a light side. Sometimes the shadow side predominates for any one of a thousand reasons. T.S. Eliot in 'The Hollow Men' writes:

> Between the idea
> And the reality
> Between the motion
> And the act
> Falls the shadow
>
> Between the conception
> And the creation
> Between the emotion
> And the response
> Falls the shadow.[4]

It's as if we are being invited to enter or face head-on the negative or dark side within us and allow it to be transformed. But we're afraid, because between the 'idea' of love and the reality falls the shadow of hatred; between the idea of pardon and the reality falls the shadow of the injury done to us; between the idea of faith and the reality of believing falls the shadow of crippling doubt; between the idea of hope and the reality of being hope bearers falls the shadow of despair; between the idea of light and its shining reality falls the shadow of the darkness from which we long to emerge; between the idea of joy and its experiential reality falls the shadow of sadness; between the conception or the planting of the tiniest seed of any one of these wonderful fruits and their actual ripening or maturing falls the shadow of hard growth and testing; between the positive emotion that can be very fleeting, especially if we've been through or are currently experiencing a hard time, and the response that we know is the right one to make falls the shadow of the other side of the coin.

Where there is hatred, let me sow love. That's the first signpost or marker in the process! We are no strangers to hatred, whether we admit it or not. The old adage that hatred and love are two sides of the one coin is true. It is so easy if something is out of kilter within us for us to tip over into hatred. Very often the chief target is the self. Self-hatred is one of the most destructive forces, not only for our own being but for others with whom we come into contact. When we find it very difficult to love ourselves, then the consequences of that difficulty can have devastating effects on those around us, both in our reactions to them and our behaviour towards them. It was Nietzsche who said, 'Do not gaze too long into the abyss lest the abyss gaze into you'. There is a sense in which we can 'become' our hatred. If we dwell on it too long, it becomes the place of familiarity, the place where we feel at home. It is at that point that the abyss has started to gaze into us – and we are trapped by this powerful negative emotion. This can happen not only to individuals, but to communities and, indeed, to whole nations. It is true also for all the other places of shadow mentioned in this prayer – doubt, despair, darkness and sadness. And when we cannot face what is within, then we project it outwards upon others.

Lord, make me! How do we let the process of transformation begin? Well, first of all, we have to desire it. God honours the desire of our hearts. If the desire to be 'made' or moulded is there, even if we can't seem to translate it into any sort of action, then the Holy Spirit is given permission to work. At first that work may seem to lead us into greater chaos, into the wilderness (as the Spirit did Jesus), the place of madness or temptation, the place, maybe for us, of greater hatred or doubt or darkness. And we will resist it. We will want to turn back to the old securities. We will be consumed by a fear of the unknown and it may seem to us as if God is playing games with us, that he is hiding himself. It can, indeed, be a lonesome valley. We cling to the old, because how would we cope if there was no more hatred to fuel the negative energy within us or justify behaviour that stems from self-loathing? How do we stand up to the hatred within and the hatred that we encounter outside of ourselves? How could we begin to live with the rather frightening and overwhelming truth that we are totally and unconditionally loved? What would we do with the space left within us as a result of letting go of old injuries and grudges and allowing forgiveness to flow? What would happen if we permitted ourselves to be carried along on a river of pardon? Would something in us rebel or resent that others were being let off the hook, or perhaps the more frightening possibility that we ourselves were to be let off the hook, because the very last person we would seek to forgive would be 'this self'. Would we lose a very convenient hiding place if doubt were removed? Not that doubt would disappear. It is part of the struggle towards maturity that lasts a lifetime. If it ceased to be the controlling force that it once was, it could become a rather stark gift that highlights and strengthens our faith as we struggle with it rather than give in.

Despair is one of the all-pervading diseases of our time. Those who are bearers of hope are regarded by secular society at best with some degree of cynicism, at worst as deluded fools living in a world of make-believe. Hope, which is not to be confused with an easy or superficial optimism, is one of the biggest gifts that Christians have to offer this present age. So much of what is happening in the world can leave us feeling totally helpless. A common reaction is to simply switch off, because it's all too overwhelming. If we don't think about it, or don't listen to the news, if we bury our heads in the sand and batten down the hatches, it all may go away. Where do we stand in relation to hope? Despair can suck us in so easily. Is our yearning for hope such that we are willing to become its prisoners? What would it take for us to resolve that never again will we give in to despair and to underwrite that resolution with our lives?

Darkness can be frightening, disorientating, even sinister. It can rob us of so much, perhaps especially rob us of vision, of destiny, of purpose. And yet darkness can lose its power over us simply by a pinprick of light, by one flickering little flame. Why keep waiting for some other power or impersonal authority to turn on a floodlight, that we vainly hope will dispel all darkness, when we already carry within us the light that no darkness, no power cut, no act of terrorism can ever extinguish? If each of us brought that little bit of light that burns within us together, across all man-made divisions, we, as the Church of Jesus Christ, would be a force to be reckoned with, instead of an institution largely dismissed as being increasingly irrelevant.

St Francis had a great many reasons to be discouraged, yet one of his chief attributes, perhaps the one that draws us to him the most and yet, paradoxically for us, is the most elusive, was joy. Richard Rohr says of him that 'he was quintessentially a man in love, and a man in love with the greatest of lovers. There was simply no bottom to his grateful happiness. He told his friars that it was their vocation to lift up peoples' hearts and give them reasons for spiritual joy. They needed no other justification for their life. They needed no other ministry in the Church. They, like he, were to be troubadours and minstrels of the Lord.'[5] Joy is very hard to define. It is probably the most selfless of all the emotions. We find it much easier to commiserate with someone in their sadness than to unselfishly rejoice in their good fortune. And where there is great sadness, we feel totally ill-equipped and inadequate to enter that sadness. At best we come with an embarrassed silence, at worst with pious platitudes. But to press through the heavy shadows of sadness and bring joy – where would we begin? Very simply put, if Jesus is first in our lives, others second and ourselves last, then we have joy. This was so true for St Francis. The more he fell in love with the Great Lover, the more he was propelled in love towards those whose hearts were in anguish, whose spirits were oppressed, whose bodies were broken, and the greater joy he experienced.

Lord, make me an instrument of your peace. In order to be such an instrument we require to be transformed, to move out of the safe places, which are often places of shadow. We are challenged to face some uncomfortable realities within ourselves and then invited to do some unfamiliar, even risky things, where the shadows fall for others. This is our challenge, to walk the road that Jesus walked, a journey that may initially lead us into chaos, but as we are 'forced' or persuaded by the Spirit to let go, then the power of love quenches the smouldering embers or even the blazing fire of hatred; the continuous flow of pardon washes away the dividing wall of injury; the life-giving energy of faith does to death the demons of doubt; the standard of hope is raised irrevocably over the defeated battle grounds of despair; unquenchable light pierces the darkness of sin, of death and of evil; and joy wells up and dances its way, rainbow-like, through the greyness of years and tears of sadness. We are in the process of transformation, of being the change we want to see in our world. But it is important not to discount the process of walking through the shadows. There are treasures hidden there that we wouldn't find anywhere else. Because of Jesus, the shadows will not have the last say. He has entered the shadows for us. His letting-go required him to be nailed to a cross. His entering the centre of chaos brings us the peace of which he now asks us to become instruments.

O Divine Master, grant that I may not so much seek
to be consoled as to console;
to be understood as to understand;
to be loved as to love.

Just as negative emotions and harmful feelings can become addictive and very destructive, so too positive thoughts, generous actions and compassionate reactions can become a way of life that, once we familiarise ourselves with this perhaps strange and new territory, there is no turning back. In the process of letting go and daring to set out as a pilgrim to a new world, that of the upside-down Kingdom of God, there comes a point where we cross the Rubicon. We may have been plunged into chaos and wilderness wanderings. We may even have felt that we were bordering on the edges of madness. We may have walked through the dark ravine and felt utterly abandoned, but we are not the people we were. There's still a lot of transforming to be done. There may be more chaos, more moving out from safe places, more stretching. That will never stop this side of death, but our certainties now are different, our trust is more secure, our goal is more clearly defined. Our world may even have been turned upside down, but only in order that we may fulfil our calling as those who themselves turn the world upside down – for Jesus' sake. How do we do that?

St Francis gives us, yet again, the key. When we are hurting, grieving, feeling abandoned in our particular anguish, the immediate, instinctive reaction is to cry out for help, for comfort, for consolation. When we are in a place of isolation or rejection, put there by the misunderstanding of others, we are desperate for someone to counter the act of betrayal, to stand with us in that sense of dereliction, to understand us, to take our story seriously and to award us the dignity and respect of being really heard. When we are in a space where we feel that we are unlovable – and we've all been there – or where our whole beings are parched for the want of not only knowing that we are loved but feeling it as well, we yearn for what we believe is the impossible, namely a sensitive and gentle rescue operation that will lead us out from the shadowlands of 'no love' to the wonder of being the beloved. When we are wounded, we become the victim. We pick up the mantle of victimhood. It is perhaps acceptable to remain there for a little while. In fact, it is important to fully recognise the hurt, because only then can we begin to do something about it. The problem arises when we make victimhood our home. Very quickly other uninvited guests can take up residence within us – like resentment, bitterness, self-pity and a desire for revenge (which we can misname 'justice'). In the natural world, this seems perfectly logical and permissible, but if we are seeking to be followers of Jesus, it's simply not. That may seem to be very harsh – but who ever said that following would be easy? Nobody escapes being hurt, even deeply wounded in and by life. That's inevitable, especially if we're seeking to really live as opposed to merely existing. But it's what we do with the pain, with the wounding that makes the difference. It can help make us or we can allow it to destroy us. If we see it as something that nurtures our spirituality, even at the cost of pain, then we have the sometimes stark but, paradoxically, ever joyful company on the road of the One whose wounds bring us healing and whose passion, death and resurrection become the instrument of our peace. Then we, in turn, can be channels of that peace to others.

Jesus, during the three short years of his public ministry, with his passionate commitment, never stopped healing, forgiving, comforting, listening – and challenging. In his humanity, he had the same heart's desire for consolation, to know that he mattered to another human being, especially in the times of sadness, grief, temptation and loss. How much he ached to be understood, that people would look and see, would hear and understand the good news he embodied. He needed love and human companionship, perhaps especially on that final journey to Jerusalem when he knew what lay ahead for him. If we don't grasp that – the humanity of Jesus as well as his divinity – then we have missed the whole point. He didn't allow his own deep need to be consoled, to be understood, to be loved, to take precedence over the needs of others. As we sow the seeds mentioned in the first part of the prayer of St Francis, we are in the process of being 'made' by Jesus into an instrument of his peace. The next stage of the journey is this, and if we have sowed faithfully and with integrity, then this activity will follow almost naturally – or should I say, supernaturally? Through sowing love, pardon, faith, hope, light and joy, not once, but again and again and again, we will one day recognise that there is a transforming power at work within us. Self has been mastered to the extent that we can respond to the needs of others, even when we ourselves are going through a tough time, a dark valley, an anguish of the soul. This does not mean that we become a doormat ready to soak up the dirt of everybody's demands or wants. What it does mean is that even in the midst of our own need, we can be present for others in theirs. We can even, when occasion demands it, put the self right off the agenda. There are times when we do need to seek consolation for ourselves, when we do have to experience some understanding – to have someone 'stand under' the essence of who we are, when we know ourselves to be the beloved. As we walk with Jesus, we will come to discern when those times are and when they are simply a desire to have our own wants gratified before we reach out to others.

To console means to bring comfort in a time of sadness or distress. There are as many ways of bringing comfort as there are people. It may involve listening, or simply being present without words. It could mean practical help, even a continuously repeated action over a period of time. It certainly will involve commitment, otherwise it will not be trusted and the sadness or distress of the other will be worsened rather than relieved. It can also mean giving courage to another to keep on going in a difficult situation. In the early Church, there was a lovely character whose name was Joseph. The apostles nicknamed him Barnabas, which means (in the old translations) the 'son of consolation'. In the newer versions it is translated the 'son of encouragement'. He allowed himself to be 'made' by God. One of the ways he sought to console, to encourage was to sell a field he owned and bring the money to the apostles for those who were in need.

Sometimes we crave to be understood. It is one of the loneliest places to be, the place where you feel no one understands you. To realise or grasp where a person is coming from, to see their side of a particular situation, to listen to their story, to know or to sense what is happening to them and why they find themselves where they are at a particular point in time is one of the greatest gifts we can give to another. It involves a deep and active listening (which can be very hard work), a recognition of a common humanity and the resulting dignity that flows from it, a respect for the other (even or especially if they are different or we disagree with them). It means to affirm someone in their personhood, to hold in a freeing and open way the essence of who they are. If anyone has ever done that for you, you will know what I mean.

It was love that drove Jesus. And for him love was a decision, the hard choice. It was love that drove him up the steep hill of Calvary and it was love that kept him nailed to the cross until love was triumphant. St Francis was a man in love with the greatest of lovers. It was love, the love of Jesus for him, that undergirded and inspired all he did and who he was. But he was no sentimental or romantic fool, although he was regarded as such by some. He knew that love was more a decision than a feeling. I'm sure he didn't 'feel' like kissing the lepers or sharing their food from the same bowl into which they dipped their bleeding, oozing fingers. I'm sure the thought of begging for crusts in the streets of his home town of Assisi, from the rich who were his one-time companions, didn't immediately fill him with delight. But each time he made the decision to love in this way, the feeling followed afterwards. He was filled with joy. He actively sought out the unlovable and shocked them with the totality of his love, his acceptance, his caring. He didn't wait to be loved. He went out from the place of comfort and security and opened his arms in love to the world, especially the world of the poor. In doing so, he was following closely in the footsteps of his master. Can we pray like this and live out what we have prayed? Surely it is asking too much? St Paul, writing to the believers in Corinth, says this: 'When we see that you're just as willing to endure the hard times as to enjoy the good times, we know you're going to make it, no doubt about it.'[6] Can we pray such a prayer? Can we be such a bridge? I believe we can!

Notes

1   Elizabeth Goudge, *St Francis of Assisi* (London: Hodder and Stoughton Ltd, 1961), pp. 13–14.

2   Richard Rohr and John Feister, *Hope Against Darkness* (Cincinnati, OH: St Anthony Messenger Press, 2001), pp. 120–1.

3   Quoted in Elizabeth Goudge, *St Francis of Assisi*, p. 263.

4   T.S. Eliot 'The Hollow Men', *Poems 1909–1925* (London: Faber & Faber, 1932), p. 123.

5   Richard Rohr and John Feister, *Hope Against Darkness*, p. 118.

6   Scripture quotation taken from *The Message*.

CHAPTER ELEVEN

Between the End and the Beginning

What we call the beginning is often the end.
And to make an end is to make a beginning.
The end is where we start from[1]

To be an instrument of God's peace, to be a bridge, is the greatest calling on any person of faith. It is not for the faint-hearted. In the end it will cost everything, but that need not be a negative or a terrifying prospect. The process of being made or moulded into such an instrument will last a lifetime, and even then there's more! But God takes us at a pace that he knows we can cope with, even if we think it's too much. We are not 'made' or transformed all at once. And there are blessings, rewards, even joy along the way – eternity moments that keep us going. The prayer of St Francis is a pilgrimage, a journey. We move from the main petition that we be made, by the Lord, into instruments of his peace through the work, the transforming that needs to take place within ourselves, in order that we may sow the seeds of peace in all areas of discord or disharmony. We then find ourselves in the upside-down Kingdom of God, where things as we have known them or expected them to operate are somehow turned on their head. God's agenda begins to take over from the world's agenda and it leads us to some surprising places and encounters and demands a different way of reacting. We have made the decision to follow, to walk this particular road that at times will be a costly one to travel.

And then, at the end, we reach the blessing or the reward which is, in reality, a new beginning.

> For it is in giving that we receive;
> It is in pardoning that we are pardoned;
> And it is in dying that we are born to eternal life.

Each phrase is really saying the same thing in a different way. It's all about letting go and about the mystery of not knowing the consequence until we have actually done it. It is more in the letting go, the surrender, rather than the holding on, that our spirituality is forged. That is where trust comes in, big time! A beginning is only possible when we make an end. We resist, sometimes to the bitter (and it can be bitter) end, the letting go, whereas, if we had done it with a joyous abandon, as St Francis did all those years ago in front of the bishop and his irate father, we would be blessed much sooner! There are different kinds of giving, of letting go. If we give in order somehow to have power over a situation or other people, if we seek to be in control, then we're not going to receive. We're going to take. Our giving, as everything else, must stem from love. It is when we give without calculation, without seeking any return on our gift, that we can be surprised by joy and can learn how to be receivers rather than takers. We often wait for the other person to make the first move, especially in the whole area of forgiveness, feeling justified because it is we who have been hurt the most. God freely offers us his forgiveness, but sometimes we don't experience it or 'feel' as if we have been forgiven. One of the meanings of the word is to 'give something before'. 'It is in pardoning that we are pardoned.' It is not that God doesn't want to forgive us, but if we are holding resentment, grudges or unforgiveness in our hearts, then somehow the flow of God's forgiveness is obstructed, not from his side but from ours.

In refusing to forgive, we are putting ourselves into a place of exile, a no-man's-land. It doesn't alter God's love for us, but in order for him to be true 'to his name', he isn't free to act towards us in the way that he would like. Mutual forgiveness is to be one of the chief hallmarks of God's kingdom and is probably the most powerful and yet the most unexplored and under-used spiritual force available to us as we seek to live between the times. If beginnings emerge from endings, then forgiveness is the key.

We fight death so much, don't we? Not just physical death, but the death of the familiar, what we've been used to. Yet transformation has to do with dying, dying to the old self, entering the chaos and emerging into something new, a type of resurrection. Eternal life is not something that begins at some vague point after death. It is something that can begin right now, in this moment, when we let go of some of the old and often negative securities, and enter the unknown – with God.

While writing this, I have received another letter from my old friend in Holland. In it he says: 'I have now entered the last phase of my life in a home of priests in retirement. It is a powerful invitation to abandonment, the end of my trust-walk with God. His name be praised!' And I am reminded so forcibly of another old 'friend' in the communion of saints, Simeon. He believed with all his heart that one day God would send his promised Messiah to come and rescue his people. He knew (because the Spirit had revealed this to him) that he would not die until he had seen the Promised One. In the in-between time, he committed himself to a life of constant prayer and faithful watchfulness. He was one of 'the quiet in the land'. His faithfulness was rewarded. When Mary and Joseph brought Jesus to the Temple, I wonder did God speak directly into the spirit of the old man with words like these: 'This is it, Simeon! This is my time. Here is my Son. He will be the light of the world and the glory of Israel although, like now, many will not recognise him. But your eyes, dear Simeon, your eyes have seen him, and blessed are you.' With the eyes of faith he recognised the moment. He was fully aware. He didn't care what anyone else was thinking. For those who did take him under their notice – why that was just old Simeon in the first stages of his dotage on a bit of a religious high! As his arms embraced and held this tiny life that was to become life for the world, Simeon's spirit overflowed with thankfulness and he sang his song from a full and a glad heart: 'Now Lord, let me depart in peace. As you promised, so my eyes have seen. It is enough. A Saviour not just for Israel but for the whole world! Amen! Amen!'

I am so encouraged by Simeon and Anna (who comes on the scene a little later), by Elizabeth and Zechariah, by Moses, by Abraham and Sarah, by Fr Joseph, by many of our volunteers in Restoration Ministries. My spirit is excited by the fact that while God often chooses younger people in this, the most important part of his dealings with his world, he also selects senior citizens to risk, to trust, to proclaim and to announce, with prophetic voices and lives, what God wants the world to see and hear and experience. All through the years, they have nurtured their love relationship with God. Their trust-walk with him has been tried and tested. Out of the tough experiences of life, they have forged a spirituality for between the times. Each of them wears an invisible banner that declares, 'The best is yet to be!' They have believed that so totally and have been so filled with expectancy that they have had relatively no problem in recognising his presence among them. Along with many others throughout this country and around the world, they are the 'quiet in the land', who wait patiently for God, who simply get on with the tasks in hand, but all the while their spirits are on tiptoe, passionately waiting for a new movement of the Spirit that will advance the shalom, the well-being of these weary, often self-centred islands and this ill-divided and ravaged earth. They are real 'church'. It could be that they are the ones who will be the vanguard of the new awareness that is surely coming. It could be that they are the ones who, with the eyes of faith and with courageous hearts, will lay down the old mantle of Church as we have known it for so long. It will seem like an ending, as like Simeon of old, they pray, 'Now, Lord, let us, your servants, depart in peace'. But their eyes will have seen and they will know that what they have called the end is really a beginning.

Long ago, the prophet Isaiah wrote of the coming reign of God, 'Then the eyes of the blind shall be opened and the ears of the deaf unstopped; then the lame shall leap like a deer and the tongue of the speechless sing for joy. For waters shall break forth in the wilderness and streams in the desert' (Isa 35:5-6; NRSV). This is a time when we need to trust enough to keep on journeying, even when we don't see the way ahead too clearly. It is a time when we affirm the promises of God that the wilderness period which we, as the Church, have known, is going to be transformed into rejoicing and that the desert places in our community life are going to blossom like the rose. We have good news to share, in spite of so much evidence to the contrary, news that is going to strengthen tired hands and encourage weak knees and give strength to those who have been imprisoned by fear for far too long. And the good news is that our God is coming. In the midst of so much that would seek to drag us back to old ways of acting and reacting, our God is coming to save us, to destroy our enemies. What are those enemies? They are certainly not other human beings, created in his image and likeness. Their names are legion. Included in their ranks are despair, doubt, cynicism, injustice, sectarianism, bitterness, racism, guilt and fear. When he comes, he will open the eyes of the blind and unstop the ears of the deaf. Those who have been blinded for years, maybe ancestrally for centuries, are going to begin to see, to recognise the other who is different as their sister, their brother. Those who have not been able to hear another's truth because they have been deafened by the programmed slogans of their own tribe or by their own self-righteousness are going to have the ears of their hearts unstopped. When he comes, the lame will leap like a deer and those who cannot speak will shout and sing. Those whose spirits have been bent over and crippled from years of abuse and injustice are going to stand up and walk tall in a new-found identity as beloved daughters and sons of God. Those who have been silenced, who have had no one to listen to the cry of their heart are going to sing a song of freedom from their broken places that the whole world will hear. The parched land of our own littleness of purpose and narrowness of vision and meanness of spirit is going to be swamped by the overflowing grace and love of a generous-hearted God, and the Spirit of God, welling up like springs of water will satisfy the thirsty souls of those who have long been yearning for something that material possessions could not satisfy.

As the years progress, the outer circumstances may change. The essential calling doesn't. It's just that, for those with a deep commitment to follow – that is, not only to believe but to follow – we are being taken deeper. The challenge to be instruments of his peace is more profound, more all-embracing and has consequences that we might never have imagined when we started out – for our own lives and the lives of those around us. One of the best-known quotations from St Francis comes as he is nearing the end of his earthly journey. He says to his brothers – and sisters – 'Let us begin again, for up to now we have done nothing.'[2] That's a good place to be. I pray that, for as long as God keeps us in being, we will always find ourselves in that space. It's the place of humility, of grace, of love, of hope. It is the place of resurrection and open doors and new opportunities, a place where we can pray

with ever-increasing desire and conviction, 'Lord, make me ...'
And as we look back to tomorrow, may we be continually graced
with that awareness that God is choosing us now and now and
now.

Notes

1   T.S. Eliot 'Little Gidding', *Four Quartets*, p. 47.
2   St Francis of Assisi. Quoted in Richard Rohr and John Feister, *Hope Against Darkness*, p. 120.

Prayer

Lord, this day belongs to you, this world belongs to you and we belong to you.

For this we give you thanks.

You call us to make a difference in your world.

While we give you thanks for such an awesome calling, we need to tell you that sometimes we find it difficult.

It is sometimes hard to be a bridge.

It is sometimes lonely to truly live between the times.

It is sometimes hard to see an old dispensation slipping away when the new has not yet come into view.

Yet, in the midst of hardness, loneliness and sadness, you call us to rejoice.

You walk with us through times of uncertainty.

You are with us in our endings and in our beginnings.

You are our centre.

As you have made a difference in our lives, we affirm that we will go where you direct.

We will be a bridge between the times.

We will be prisoners of hope.

And we will never give up.

> Amen.

Acknowledgements

I would like to thank the Board of Directors of Restoration Ministries for giving me sabbatical time to write this book; also Rose and all the friends of the ministry for their encouragement and prayers. Richard Kennedy and Eithne Agnew were invaluable in their painstaking proofreading and correcting. To the SMA community at Dromantine near Newry, Co. Down, for their warm welcome, generous hospitality and quiet friendship as I worked – a thousand thanks. Dromantine, and its beautiful setting, was truly holy ground and I felt blessed to be there. I am indebted to Jean Vanier, Nuala O'Loan and Trevor Williams for their endorsements of this book. Thank you, too, to Maura Hyland, Director of Veritas who suggested the topic, to Caitriona Clarke and Donna Doherty for their help and encouragement, and to all the team at Veritas for their constant availability and support.